THE LOVE BOOK

♡

No words could ever really translate all that I feel for you in my heart darling x This is a collection of writing that in part reflects the wonder of love that I am blessed to experience with you x

All my love, my Gorgeous Valentine

xXxx (2015)

ALSO BY ALLIE ESIRI

If: A Treasury of Poems for Almost Every Possibility

Allie Esiri read Modern and Medieval Languages at St Catharine's College, Cambridge. An actress from 1989–2000, she then worked as a freelance writer for publications including American *Vogue* and *The New York Times*. Allie conceived and co-created the *iF Poems* app, its accompanying anthology *iF: A Treasury Of Poems For Almost Every Possibility* and more recently *The Love Book* app, with readings by Gina Bellman, Helena Bonham Carter, Tom Hiddleston, Damian Lewis, Helen McCrory and Emma Watson.

CLASSIC AND CONTEMPORARY POEMS,

LETTERS AND PROSE ON THE WONDERFUL

(BUT TROUBLESOME) THEME OF LOVE

■ SQUARE PEG

To M.L.V.E.

Published by Square Peg 2014

2 4 6 8 10 9 7 5 3 1

Introduction copyright © Allie Esiri 2014

Please see p.233 for poetry copyrights and acknowledgements

The moral rights of the author have been asserted

First published in Great Britain in 2014 by Square Peg
Random House, 20 Vauxhall Bridge Road, London SW1V 2SA

www.vintage-books.co.uk

Addresses for companies within The Random House Group Limited
can be found at: www.randomhouse.co.uk/offices.htm

The Random House Group Limited Reg. No. 954009

A CIP catalogue record for this book is available from the British Library

ISBN 9780224098939

The Random House Group Limited supports the Forest Stewardship
Council® (FSC®), the leading international forest-certification organisation. Our
books carrying the FSC label are printed on FSC®-certified paper. FSC is the only
forest-certification scheme supported by the leading environmental organisations,
including Greenpeace. Our paper procurement policy can be found at
www.randomhouse.co.uk/environment

Mixed Sources
Product group from well-managed
forests and other controlled sources
www.fsc.org Cert no. TT-COC-2139
© 1996 Forest Stewardship Council

Designed and produced by The Curved House/Emma King

Printed and bound in Italy by Graphicom

❦ FOREWORD ❧

It's not easy to write a foreword for a book about love. The hardest thing is avoiding the clichés. They are everywhere, like drunk uncles at a wedding. Love is blind; love is all you need; love is all around; love means never having to say you're sorry; love, love, love; let's do it, let's fall in love; love is a many-splendored thing. It really is one of the most abused four-letter words in the English language.

But this is precisely why love needs a book of poetry. To save it from all this. Because no one can express love more eloquently or elegantly than the poet. Auden defined the poet as 'a person who is passionately in love with language'. True mastery is required to convey the emotion that is so central to all our lives and so prone to chocolate-box hyperbole.

There are times when only the poet can rescue us. Wouldn't we all like to have Shakespeare hiding behind the plant pot on our first date? Or consoling us with fine words over a broken appointment.

My first encounter with the power of poetry was at the age of 16, struggling to make sense of falling in love for the first time. A friend introduced me to John Clare's 'First Love' – "My heart has left its dwelling-place/ And can return no more" – and I felt as though someone understood me. I felt as though the lines had been written for me and me alone, salve for my own special agony.

That, of course, is the mark of a great writer.

Love is the most complex of emotions, since it encompasses so many others: joy, jealousy, passion, grief, terror, loss. It comes, too, in many forms: *storge*, *philia*, *eros*, *agape* – Greek terms for familial affection, friendship, sexual desire and love "that seeketh not to please". It is a universal experience, one familiar to us all, and it is this universality that I have tried to express in my choice of poems. Within each chapter, the authors of the poems and love letters have been ordered (loosely) chronologically.

They are – I hope – all very accessible. They will appeal to the novice as much as the expert. They all contain elements of the familiar, whether it be the stone hands of lovers clasped in eternal union in Philip Larkin's 'An Arundel Tomb' or the simple sorrow of loss and longing in George MacDonald's two-line exhortation, 'The Shortest and Sweetest of Songs' – perhaps the only poem ever written with a title that's longer than itself.

This is not the last word in literature about love. It is simply an anthology, an expression of my lifelong love of poetry.

Allie Esiri, February 2014

CONTENTS

If it's Love

The Comparison by CATULLUS   3

A letter from HENRY VIII to ANNE BOLEYN   4

The Face That Launched A Thousand Ships, from *Dr Faustus:*
    Act V Scene I by CHRISTOPHER MARLOWE   5

Sonnet 130 (My mistress' eyes are nothing like the sun)
    by WILLIAM SHAKESPEARE   6

Sonnet 18 (Shall I compare thee to a summer's day?)
    by WILLIAM SHAKESPEARE   7

From *Romeo and Juliet: Act 3 Scene 2* by WILLIAM SHAKESPEARE   8

To Celia by BEN JONSON   9

From *The Song of Solomon*, THE KING JAMES BIBLE   10

She Walks in Beauty by GEORGE GORDON, LORD BYRON   11

A letter from GEORGE GORDON, LORD BYRON to COUNTESS TERESA GUICCIOLI   12

I hid my love when young till I by JOHN CLARE   13

Bright Star by JOHN KEATS   14

Sonnet 38 (First time he kissed me) by ELIZABETH BARRETT BROWNING   15

A letter from JOHN KEATS to FANNY BRAWNE   16

To Helen by EDGAR ALLAN POE   18

O tan-faced prairie-boy by WALT WHITMAN   19

When I heard at the close of the day by WALT WHITMAN   20

Silent Noon by DANTE GABRIEL ROSSETTI   21

A Birthday by CHRISTINA ROSSETTI   22

It was a quiet way by EMILY DICKINSON   23

A Drinking Song by W.B. YEATS   24

Conviction (iv) by STEVIE SMITH   25

Lullaby by W.H AUDEN   26

I Knew a Woman by THEODORE ROETHKE   28

Close close all night, from *Edgar Allan Poe & the Jukebox*
    by ELIZABETH BISHOP   29

Valentine by JOHN FULLER   30

Come. And Be My Baby by MAYA ANGELOU   33

The Orange by WENDY COPE   34

Valentine by CAROL ANN DUFFY   35

Words, Wide Night by CAROL ANN DUFFY   36

If Passionate

Doing, a filthy pleasure is, and short by PETRONIUS — 39

The Passionate Shepherd to His Love by CHRISTOPHER MARLOWE — 40

The Good Morrow by JOHN DONNE — 41

To His Coy Mistress by ANDREW MARVELL — 42

Upon Julia's Clothes by ROBERT HERRICK — 44

A letter from NAPOLEON BONAPARTE to JOSÉPHINE DE BEAUHARNAIS — 45

Lochinvar by SIR WALTER SCOTT — 46

Desire by SAMUEL TAYLOR COLERIDGE — 48

Love's Philosophy by PERCY BYSSHE SHELLEY — 49

To Fanny by JOHN KEATS — 50

Now sleeps the crimson petal by ALFRED, LORD TENNYSON — 51

Now by ROBERT BROWNING — 52

Meeting at Night by ROBERT BROWNING — 53

From *Wuthering Heights* by EMILY BRONTË — 54

To a Stranger by WALT WHITMAN — 55

A Glimpse by WALT WHITMAN — 56

Her breast is fit for pearls by EMILY DICKINSON — 57

Wild nights – Wild nights! by EMILY DICKINSON — 58

Love and Sleep by ALGERNON CHARLES SWINBURNE — 59

Leda and the Swan by W.B. YEATS — 60

A Decade by AMY LOWELL — 61

A letter from VIRGINIA WOOLF to VITA SACKVILLE-WEST — 62

From *Orlando* by VIRGINIA WOOLF — 63

New Year's Eve by D.H. LAWRENCE — 64

A letter from KATHERINE MANSFIELD to JOHN MIDDLETON MURRY — 65

From *My Diary, July 1914* by WILFRED OWEN — 66

On the Marriage of a Virgin by DYLAN THOMAS — 67

Bride and Groom Lie Hidden For Three Days by TED HUGHES — 68

The Bed by THOM GUNN — 70

Coupling by FLEUR ADCOCK — 71

Trysts by ROBIN ROBERTSON — 72

If it's A Promise

The Bargain by SIR PHILIP SIDNEY 75

Sonnet 116 (Let me not to the marriage of true minds)
    by WILLIAM SHAKESPEARE 76

Lovers' Infiniteness by JOHN DONNE 77

From *The Song of Solomon*, THE KING JAMES BIBLE 78

I Corinthians 13 from THE KING JAMES BIBLE 79

To My Dear and Loving Husband by ANNE BRADSTREET 80

A letter from WOLFGANG AMADEUS MOZART to CONSTANZE MOZART 81

A Red, Red Rose by ROBERT BURNS 82

Sonnet 14 (If thou must love me) by ELIZABETH BARRETT BROWNING 83

Sonnet 43 (How do I love thee?) by ELIZABETH BARRETT BROWNING 84

The Owl and the Pussycat by EDWARD LEAR 85

Dover Beach by MATTHEW ARNOLD 86

A Marriage by MARK TWAIN 88

He Wishes for the Cloths of Heaven by W.B. YEATS 89

Fidelity by D.H. LAWRENCE 90

On Marriage by KAHLIL GIBRAN 92

A Dedication To My Wife by T.S. ELIOT 93

Camomile Tea by KATHERINE MANSFIELD 94

i carry your heart with me (i carry it in by E.E. CUMMINGS 95

A letter from ZELDA SAYRE to F. SCOTT FITZGERALD 96

Scaffolding by SEAMUS HEANEY 98

Hinterhof by JAMES FENTON 99

Let me put it this way by SIMON ARMITAGE 100

The Vows by MICHAEL SYMMONS ROBERTS 101

Wedding by ALICE OSWALD 102

If Tickled

from *Much Ado About Nothing*, Act 2 Scene 3
    by WILLIAM SHAKESPEARE 105

*The Author loving these homely meats specially, viz.: Cream,
    Pancakes, Buttered Pippin-pies (laugh, good people) and Tobacco;
    writ to that worthy and virtuous gentlewoman, whom he calleth
    Mistress, as followeth* by JOHN DAVIES OF HEREFORD 106

The Flea by JOHN DONNE 107

A letter from WOLFGANG AMADEUS MOZART to his cousin
   (and probable first love) MARIANNE   108
When a Man has Married a Wife by WILLIAM BLAKE   111
A letter from G.K. CHESTERTON to his fiancée FRANCES BLOGG   112
To – by THOMAS MOORE   114
Recuerdo by EDNA ST VINCENT MILLAY   115
Symptom Recital by DOROTHY PARKER   116
One Perfect Rose by DOROTHY PARKER   117
may i feel said he by E.E. CUMMINGS   118
A Subaltern's Love Song by JOHN BETJEMAN   120
In the Night by STEVIE SMITH   122
Life Story by TENNESSEE WILLIAMS   123
No Loser, No Weeper by MAYA ANGELOU   124
Celia, Celia by ADRIAN MITCHELL   125
Valentine by WENDY COPE   126
Mrs Icarus by CAROL ANN DUFFY   127
Things That Could Happen by JACOB SAM-LA ROSE   128

If Thwarted

Mother, I cannot mind my wheel by SAPPHO   133
Westron wind, when will thou blow by ANONYMOUS   134
Whoso list to hunt by SIR THOMAS WYATT   135
The Nymph's Reply to the Shepherd by SIR WALTER RALEIGH   136
Sonnet 98 (From you I have been absent in the spring)
   by WILLIAM SHAKESPEARE   137
The Definition of Love by ANDREW MARVELL   138
Thrice Toss These Oaken Ashes by THOMAS CAMPION   140
The Sick Rose by WILLIAM BLAKE   141
She lay all naked by ANONYMOUS   142
Never Seek to Tell thy Love by WILLIAM BLAKE   144
Oh, Dear! What Can The Matter Be? by ANONYMOUS   145
La Belle Dame sans Merci by JOHN KEATS   146
To Mary by JOHN CLARE   148
Longing by MATTHEW ARNOLD   149
The Shortest and Sweetest of Songs by GEORGE MACDONALD   150
If you were coming in the fall by EMILY DICKINSON   151
A letter from GENERAL (DAVID) GRIER to ANNA GRIER   152
A Thunderstorm in Town by THOMAS HARDY   155
A Broken Appointment by THOMAS HARDY   156

From *Tess of the D'Urbevilles* by THOMAS HARDY 157

A letter from OSCAR WILDE to LORD ALFRED DOUGLAS 158

The Cap and Bells by W.B YEATS 160

The Love Song of St. Sebastian by T.S. ELIOT 162

Call It a Good Marriage by ROBERT GRAVES 164

Lament over Love by LANGSTON HUGHES 165

Boots of Spanish Leather by BOB DYLAN 166

Into My Arms by NICK CAVE, from the album *The Boatman's Call* 168

Talking in Bed by PHILIP LARKIN 170

If it's Over

So we'll go no more a roving by GEORGE GORDON, LORD BYRON 173

When We Two Parted by GEORGE GORDON, LORD BYRON 174

When the lamp is shattered by PERCY BYSSHE SHELLEY 175

Neutral Tones by THOMAS HARDY 176

He would not stay for me; and who can wonder? by A.E. HOUSMAN 177

Down by the Salley Gardens by W.B. YEATS 178

O Do Not Love Too Long by W.B. YEATS 179

When You Are Old by W.B. YEATS 180

'Go now' by EDWARD THOMAS 181

Will You Come? by EDWARD THOMAS 182

On Joy and Sorrow from *The Prophet* by KAHLIL GIBRAN 183

Sonnet II (Time does not bring Relief; you all have Lied)
 by EDNA ST VINCENT MILLAY 184

Ebb by EDNA ST VINCENT MILLAY 185

One Cigarette by EDWIN MORGAN 186

Animals by FRANK O'HARA 187

Pain I Did Not by SHARON OLDS 188

If Platonic

Sonnet 104 (To me, fair friend, you never can be old)
 by WILLIAM SHAKESPEARE 191

Travelling by WILLIAM WORDSWORTH 192

To Wordsworth by PERCY BYSSHE SHELLEY 193

To a Friend Who Sent Me Some Roses by JOHN KEATS 194

The Arrow And The Song by HENRY WADSWORTH LONGFELLOW 195

Love and Friendship by EMILY BRONTË   196

Sonnet: I Thank You by HENRY TIMROD   197

Polonius' Advice To His Son – paraphrased from *Hamlet*, by MARK TWAIN   198

Go to the limits of your longing by RAINER MARIA RILKE   199

And You, Helen by EDWARD THOMAS   200

From *The Velveteen Rabbit* by MARGERY WILLIAMS   201

At First Sight by ROBERT GRAVES   202

Friendship by ELIZABETH JENNINGS   203

Love after Love by DEREK WALCOTT   204

If Mourning

Sonnet 55 (Not marble, nor the gilded monuments)
    by WILLIAM SHAKESPEARE   207

Sonnet 71 (No longer mourn for me when I am dead)
    by WILLIAM SHAKESPEARE   208

Upon the death of Sir Albert Morton's Wife by SIR HENRY WOTTON   209

Holy Sonnet 17 (Since she whom I lov'd hath paid her last debt)
    by JOHN DONNE   210

On My First Son by BEN JONSON   211

The last letter from LORD NELSON to LADY HAMILTON   212

Music, when soft voices die (To —) by PERCY BYSSHE SHELLEY   213

A slumber did my spirit seal by WILLIAM WORDSWORTH   214

Song: I had a dove by JOHN KEATS   215

Sonnet 20 (Beloved, my Beloved) by ELIZABETH BARRETT BROWNING   216

From *In Memoriam A.H.H.* by ALFRED, LORD TENNYSON   217

On the Death of Anne Brontë by CHARLOTTE BRONTË   218

To One Shortly To Die by WALT WHITMAN   219

Remember by CHRISTINA ROSSETTI   220

Song by CHRISTINA ROSSETTI   221

Rain on a Grave by THOMAS HARDY   222

The Voice by THOMAS HARDY   224

Along the fields as we came by BY A.E. HOUSMAN   225

From a sermon in May 1910 following the death of King Edward VII
    titled *Death the King of Terrors* by HENRY SCOTT HOLLAND   226

The suicide note from VIRGINIA WOOLF to LEONARD WOOLF   227

An Arundel Tomb by PHILIP LARKIN   228

Red by TED HUGHES   230

Acknowledgements   232

Indexes   236

'I don't remember who was there, except
Dora. I have not the least idea what we had
for dinner, besides Dora. My impression
is, that I dined off Dora, entirely, and sent
away half-a-dozen plates untouched.'

CHARLES DICKENS, FROM *DAVID COPPERFIELD*

The Comparison

The crowd of beauteous Quintia prate:
To me she is but fair and straight;
So far I can comply.
Those stated charms her form displays;
But still the full, the general praise,
Of beauteous I deny.

No grain of sprightliness or grace
In all her lofty form we trace.
I Lesbia beauteous call;
Who, stealing from the lovely host
The separate charms each fair could boast,
Herself united all.

CATULLUS, TRANSLATED BY GEORGE LAMB

A letter from
Henry VIII to Anne Boleyn

My Mistress and my Friend –

My heart and I surrender themselves into your hands, and we supplicate to be commended to your good graces, and that by absence your affection may not be diminished to us, for that would be to augment our pain, which would be a great pity, since absence gives enough, and more than I ever thought could be felt. This brings to my mind a fact in astronomy, which is, that the further the poles are from the sun, notwithstanding, the more searing is the heat. Thus it is with our love: absence has placed distance between us, nevertheless, fervour increases, at least on my part. I hope the same from you, assuring you that in my case the anguish of absence is so great that it would be intolerable, were it not for the firm hope I have of your indissoluble affection towards me. In order to remind you of it, and because I cannot in person be in your presence, I send you the thing that comes nearest that is possible – that is to say, my picture, and the whole device, which you already know of, set in bracelets, wishing myself in their place when it pleases you. This is from the hand of

Your servant and friend,

H.R.

Henry VIII

The Face That Launched A Thousand Ships

Was this the face that launched a thousand ships
And burnt the topless towers of Ilium?
Sweet Helen, make me immortal with a kiss;
Her lips suck forth my soul; see where it flies!–
Come, Helen, come, give me my soul again.
Here will I dwell, for heaven be in these lips,
And all is dross that is not Helena.
I will be Paris, and for love of thee,
Instead of Troy, shall Wittenberg be sack'd;
And I will combat with weak Menelaus,
And wear thy colours on my plumed crest.
Yea, I will wound Achilles in the heel
And then return to Helen for a kiss.
O, thou art fairer than the evening air,
Clad in the beauty of a thousand stars.
Brighter art thou than flaming Jupiter
When he appear'd to hapless Semele,
More lovely than the monarch of the sky
In wanton Arethusa's azured arms;
And none but thou shalt be my paramour!

**CHRISTOPHER MARLOWE,
FROM *DR FAUSTUS* (ACT V SCENE I)**

Sonnet 130

(MY MISTRESS' EYES ARE NOTHING LIKE THE SUN)

My mistress' eyes are nothing like the sun;
Coral is far more red than her lips' red;
If snow be white, why then her breasts are dun;
If hairs be wires, black wires grow on her head.
I have seen roses damasked, red and white,
But no such roses see I in her cheeks;
And in some perfumes is there more delight
Than in the breath that from my mistress reeks.
I love to hear her speak, yet well I know
That music hath a far more pleasing sound;
I grant I never saw a goddess go;
My mistress when she walks treads on the ground.
  And yet, by heaven, I think my love as rare
  As any she belied with false compare.

WILLIAM SHAKESPEARE

Sonnet 18

(SHALL I COMPARE THEE TO A SUMMER'S DAY?)

Shall I compare thee to a summer's day?
Thou art more lovely and more temperate:
Rough winds do shake the darling buds of May,
And summer's lease hath all too short a date:
Sometime too hot the eye of heaven shines,
And often is his gold complexion dimmed;
And every fair from fair sometime declines,
By chance or nature's changing course untrimmed;
But thy eternal summer shall not fade
Nor lose possession of that fair thou ow'st;
Nor shall Death brag thou wander'st in his shade,
When in eternal lines to time thou grow'st:
    So long as men can breathe or eyes can see,
    So long lives this and this gives life to thee.

WILLIAM SHAKESPEARE

from Romeo and Juliet

ACT 3 SCENE 2

JULIET: Give me my Romeo; and when I shall die,
Take him and cut him out in little stars,
And he will make the face of heaven so fine
That all the world will be in love with night,
And pay no worship to the garish sun.
O, I have bought the mansion of a love,
But not possess'd it, and though I am sold,
Not yet enjoy'd. So tedious is this day
As is the night before some festival
To an impatient child that hath new robes
And may not wear them. O, here comes my nurse,
And she brings news, and every tongue that speaks
But Romeo's name speaks heavenly eloquence.

WILLIAM SHAKESPEARE

To Celia

Drink to me only with thine eyes,
    And I will pledge with mine;
Or leave a kiss but in the cup,
    And I'll not look for wine.
The thirst that from the soul doth rise
    Doth ask a drink divine;
But might I of Jove's nectar sup,
    I would not change for thine.

I sent thee late a rosy wreath,
    Not so much honouring thee
As giving it a hope that there
    It could not withered be.
But thou thereon didst only breathe,
    And sent'st it back to me;
Since when it grows, and smells, I swear,
    Not of itself, but thee.

BEN JONSON

from The Song of Solomon

THE KING JAMES BIBLE, 1611

My beloved is white and ruddy,
the chiefest among ten thousand.
His head is as the most fine gold,
his locks are bushy, and black as a raven.
His eyes are as the eyes of doves by the rivers of water,
washed with milk, and fitly set.
His cheeks are as a bed of spices, as sweet flowers:
his lips like lilies, dropping sweet-smelling myrrh.
His hands are as gold rings set with the beryl:
his belly is as bright ivory overlaid with sapphires.
His legs are as pillars of marble, set upon sockets of fine gold:
his countenance is as Lebanon, excellent as the cedars.
His mouth is most sweet, yea, he is altogether lovely.

She Walks in Beauty

She walks in beauty, like the night
  Of cloudless climes and starry skies;
And all that's best of dark and bright
  Meet in her aspect and her eyes:
Thus mellow'd to that tender light
  Which heaven to gaudy day denies.

One shade the more, one ray the less,
  Had half impair'd the nameless grace
Which waves in every raven tress,
  Or softly lightens o'er her face;
Where thoughts serenely sweet express
  How pure, how dear their dwelling place.

And on that cheek, and o'er that brow,
  So soft, so calm, yet eloquent,
The smiles that win, the tints that glow,
  But tell of days in goodness spent,
A mind at peace with all below,
  A heart whose love is innocent!

GEORGE GORDON, LORD BYRON

A letter from George Gordon, Lord Byron to Countess Teresa Guiccioli

25 AUGUST, 1819

My dearest Teresa,

I have read this book in your garden; – my love, you were absent, or else I could not have read it. It is a favourite book of yours, and the writer was a friend of mine. You will not understand these English words, and others will not understand them, – which is the reason I have not scrawled them in Italian. But you will recognize the handwriting of him who passionately loved you, and you will divine that, over a book which was yours, he could only think of love.

In that word, beautiful in all languages, but most so in yours – Amor mio – is comprised my existence here and hereafter. I feel I exist here, and I feel I shall exist hereafter, – to what purpose you will decide; my destiny rests with you, and you are a woman, eighteen years of age, and two out of a convent. I love you, and you love me, – at least, you say so, and act as if you did so, which last is a great consolation in all events.

But I more than love you, and cannot cease to love you. Think of me, sometimes, when the Alps and ocean divide us, – but they never will, unless you wish it.

Byron

Byron met Teresa in 1819. She was the woman with whom he had the longest relationship of his life. She was also married: to a nobleman who, in his son's words, 'everybody hated'.

But Byron, a notorious womaniser, who had less than a year previously boasted that he had 'had them all & thrice as many to boot', was soon assuring her that she would be his 'last Passion'. And she proved to be; Byron died in 1824. Despite her increasingly implausible protestations that their relationship had always been chaste, Teresa never forgot Byron. Neither did her second husband, who would refer to her proudly as 'the Marquise de Boissy, my wife, formerly Byron's mistress'.

I hid my love when young till I

I hid my love when young till I
Couldn't bear the buzzing of a fly;
I hid my love to my despite
Till I could not bear to look at light;
I dare not gaze upon her face
But left her memory in each place;
Where'er I saw a wild flower lie
I kissed and bade my love goodbye.

I met her in the greenest dells,
Where dewdrops pearl the wood bluebells;
The lost breeze kissed her bright blue eye,
The bee kissed and went singing by,
A sunbeam found a passage there,
A gold chain round her neck so fair;
As secret as the wild bee's song
She lay there all the summer long.

I hid my love in field and town
Till e'en the breeze would knock me down;
The bees seemed singing ballads o'er,
The fly's buzz turned a lion's roar;
And even silence found a tongue,
To haunt me all the summer long;
The riddle nature could not prove
Was nothing else but secret love.

JOHN CLARE

❧ Bright Star ❧

Bright star! would I were steadfast as thou art –
    Not in lone splendour hung aloft the night
And watching, with eternal lids apart,
    Like nature's patient, sleepless Eremite,
The moving waters at their priestlike task
    Of pure ablution round earth's human shores,
Or gazing on the new soft-fallen mask
    Of snow upon the mountains and the moors –
No – yet still steadfast, still unchangeable,
    Pillowed upon my fair love's ripening breast,
To feel for ever its soft swell and fall,
    Awake for ever in a sweet unrest,
Still, still to hear her tender-taken breath,
And so live ever – or else swoon to death.

JOHN KEATS

⚘ Sonnet 38 ⚘

(FIRST TIME HE KISSED ME)

First time he kissed me, he but only kissed
The fingers of this hand wherewith I write;
And ever since, it grew more clean and white,
Slow to world-greetings, quick with its 'Oh, list,'
When the angels speak. A ring of amethyst
I could not wear here, plainer to my sight,
Than that first kiss. The second passed in height
The first, and sought the forehead, and half missed,
Half falling on the hair. O beyond meed!
That was the chrism of love, which love's own crown
With sanctifying sweetness, did precede.
The third upon my lips was folded down
In perfect, purple state; since when, indeed,
I have been proud and said, 'My love, my own.'

ELIZABETH BARRETT BROWNING

A letter from John Keats to Fanny Brawne

1820

Sweetest Fanny,

– You fear sometimes I do not love you so much as you wish? My dear Girl, I love you ever and ever and without reserve. The more I have known, the more I have lov'd. In every way, – even my jealousies have been agonies of Love; in the hottest fit I ever had I would have died for you. I have vexed you too much. But Love! Can I help it? You are always new. The last of your kisses was ever the sweetest, the last smile the brightest; the last movement the gracefullest. When you pass'd by my window home yesterday, I was fill'd with as much admiration as if I had seen you for the first time. You uttered a half complaint once that I only lov'd your beauty. Have I nothing else then to love in you but that? Do I not see a heart naturally furnish'd with wings imprison itself with me? No ill prospect has been able to turn your thoughts a moment from me. This perhaps should be as much a subject of sorrow as joy – but I will not talk of that. Even if you did not love me I could not help an entire devotion to you: how much more deeply then must I feel for you knowing you love me. My Mind has been the most discontented and restless one that ever was put into a body too small for it. I never felt my Mind repose upon anything with complete and undistracted enjoyment – upon no person but you. When you are in the room my thoughts never fly out of the window; you always concentrate my whole senses. The anxiety shown about our loves in your last note is an immense pleasure to me; however, you must not suffer such speculations to molest you any more; nor will I any more believe you can have the least pique against me. Brown is gone out – but here is Mrs Wylie – when she is gone I shall be awake for you. Remembrances to your mother. – Your affectionate,

J. Keats

Keats met Fanny when she was 18; their relationship was initially only friendly, but Fanny's compassion and understanding when Keats' younger brother died at only 19 impressed itself upon him. In a letter to his brother George, Keats described her as 'beautiful, elegant, graceful, silly, fashionable and strange'. Fanny's mother, however, withheld her consent to their marriage until such a time as Keats would be better able to support her financially.

Keats' gradual decline from tuberculosis took him to Italy in search of the warmer climate, which doctors hoped might save his life; his condition continued to worsen, however, and he died in 1821. When Fanny learnt of his death by letter, she went into a strict mourning that lasted for six years, during which time her only comfort was her correspondence with Keats' sister, also named Fanny.

To Helen

Helen, thy beauty is to me
    Like those Nicéan barks of yore
That gently, o'er a perfumed sea,
The weary, way-worn wanderer bore
To his own native shore.

On desperate seas long wont to roam,
    Thy hyacinth hair, thy classic face,
Thy Naiad airs have brought me home
    To the glory that was Greece,
And the grandeur that was Rome.

Lo! in yon brilliant window-niche
    How statue-like I see thee stand,
    The agate lamp within thy hand!
Ah, Psyche, from the regions which
    Are Holy-Land!

EDGAR ALLAN POE

O tan-faced prairie-boy

O tan-faced prairie-boy,
Before you came to camp came many a welcome gift,
Praises and presents came and nourishing food, till at last among the recruits,
You came, taciturn, with nothing to give – we but look'd on each other,
When lo! more than all the gifts of the world you gave me.

WALT WHITMAN

When I heard at the close of the day

When I heard at the close of the day how my name had been receiv'd with
plaudits in the capitol, still it was not a happy night for me that follow'd,
And else when I carous'd, or when my plans were accomplish'd, still I was not
happy,
But the day when I rose at dawn from the bed of perfect health, refresh'd,
singing, inhaling the ripe breath of autumn,
When I saw the full moon in the west grow pale and disappear in the
morning light,
When I wander'd alone over the beach, and undressing bathed, laughing
with the cool waters, and saw the sun rise,
And when I thought how my dear friend my lover was on his way coming,
O then I was happy,
O then each breath tasted sweeter, and all that day my food nourish'd me
more, and the beautiful day pass'd well,
And the next came with equal joy, and with the next at evening came my
friend,
And that night while all was still I heard the waters roll slowly continually up
the shores,
I heard the hissing rustle of the liquid and sands as directed to me
whispering to congratulate me,
For the one I love most lay sleeping by me under the same cover in the cool
night,
In the stillness in the autumn moonbeams his face was inclined toward me,
And his arm lay lightly around my breast – and that night I was happy.

WALT WHITMAN

Silent Noon

Your hands lie open in the long fresh grass, –
    The finger-points look through like rosy blooms:
    Your eyes smile peace. The pasture gleams and glooms
'Neath billowing skies that scatter and amass.
All around our nest, far as the eye can pass,
    Are golden kingcup-fields with silver edge
    Where the cow-parsley skirts the hawthorn-hedge.
'Tis visible silence, still as the hour-glass.

Deep in the sun-searched growths the dragon-fly
Hangs like a blue thread loosened from the sky: –
    So this wing'd hour is dropt to us from above.
Oh! clasp we to our hearts, for deathless dower,
This close-companioned inarticulate hour
    When twofold silence was the song of love.

DANTE GABRIEL ROSSETTI

A Birthday

My heart is like a singing bird
　Whose nest is in a water'd shoot;
My heart is like an apple-tree
　　Whose boughs are bent with thickset fruit;
My heart is like a rainbow shell
　　That paddles in a halcyon sea;
My heart is gladder than all these
　　Because my love is come to me.

Raise me a dais of silk and down;
　　Hang it with vair and purple dyes;
Carve it in doves and pomegranates,
　　And peacocks with a hundred eyes;
Work it in gold and silver grapes,
　　In leaves and silver fleurs-de-lys;
Because the birthday of my life
　　Is come, my love is come to me.

CHRISTINA ROSSETTI

It was a quiet way

It was a quiet way –
He asked if I was his –
I made no answer of the Tongue
But answer of the Eyes –
And then He bore me on
Before this mortal noise
With swiftness, as of Chariots
And distance, as of Wheels –
This World did drop away
As Acres from the feet
Of one that leaneth from Balloon
Upon an Ether street.
The Gulf behind was not,
The Continents were new –
Eternity it was before
Eternity was due –
No Seasons were to us –
It was not Night nor Morn –
But Sunrise stopped upon the place
And fastened it in Dawn –

EMILY DICKINSON

A Drinking Song

Wine comes in at the mouth
And love comes in at the eye;
That's all we shall know for truth
Before we grow old and die.
I lift the glass to my mouth,
I look at you, and I sigh.

W.B. YEATS

Conviction (iv)

I like to get off with people,
I like to lie in their arms
I like to be held and lightly kissed,
Safe from all alarms.

I like to laugh and be happy
With a beautiful kiss,
I tell you, in all the world
There is no bliss like this.

STEVIE SMITH

∾ Lullaby ∾

Lay your sleeping head, my love,
Human on my faithless arm;
Time and fevers burn away
Individual beauty from
Thoughtful children, and the grave
Proves the child ephemeral:
But in my arms till break of day
Let the living creature lie,
Mortal, guilty, but to me
The entirely beautiful.

Soul and body have no bounds:
To lovers as they lie upon
Her tolerant enchanted slope
In their ordinary swoon,
Grave the vision Venus sends
Of supernatural sympathy,
Universal love and hope;
While an abstract insight wakes
Among the glaciers and the rocks
The hermit's carnal ecstasy.

Certainty, fidelity
On the stroke of midnight pass
Like vibrations of a bell
And fashionable madmen raise
Their pedantic boring cry:
Every farthing of the cost,
All the dreaded cards foretell,
Shall be paid, but from this night
Not a whisper, not a thought,
Not a kiss nor look be lost.

Beauty, midnight, vision dies:
Let the winds of dawn that blow
Softly round your dreaming head
Such a day of welcome show
Eye and knocking heart may bless,
Find the mortal world enough;
Noons of dryness find you fed
Watched by every human love.

W.H AUDEN

I Knew a Woman

I knew a woman, lovely in her bones,
When small birds sighed, she would sigh back at them;
Ah, when she moved, she moved more ways than one:
The shapes a bright container can contain!
Of her choice virtues only gods should speak,
Or English poets who grew up on Greek
(I'd have them sing in chorus, cheek to cheek).

How well her wishes went! She stroked my chin,
She taught me Turn, and Counter-turn, and Stand;
She taught me Touch, that undulant white skin;
I nibbled meekly from her proffered hand;
She was the sickle; I, poor I, the rake,
Coming behind her for her pretty sake
(But what prodigious mowing we did make).

Love likes a gander, and adores a goose:
Her full lips pursed, the errant note to seize;
She played it quick, she played it light and loose;
My eyes, they dazzled at her flowing knees;
Her several parts could keep a pure repose,
Or one hip quiver with a mobile nose
(She moved in circles, and those circles moved).

Let seed be grass, and grass turn into hay:
I'm martyr to a motion not my own;
What's freedom for? To know eternity.
I swear she cast a shadow white as stone.
But who would count eternity in days?
These old bones live to learn her wanton ways:
(I measure time by how a body sways).

THEODORE ROETHKE

Close close all night

Close close all night
the lovers keep.
They turn together
in their sleep,

close as two pages
in a book
that read each other
in the dark.

Each knows all
the other knows,
learned by heart
from head to toes.

ELIZABETH BISHOP

Valentine

The things about you I appreciate
 May seem indelicate:
I'd like to find you in the shower
And chase the soap for half an hour.
I'd like to have you in my power
 And see your eyes dilate.
I'd like to have your back to scour
And other parts to lubricate.
Sometimes I feel it is my fate
To chase you screaming up a tower
 Or make you cower
By asking you to differentiate
 Nietzsche from Schopenhauer.
I'd like to successfully guess your weight
 And win you at a fête.
I'd like to offer you a flower.

I like the hair upon your shoulders,
Falling like water over boulders.
I like the shoulders, too: they are essential.
Your collar-bones have great potential
(I'd like all your particulars in folders
 Marked *Confidential*).

I like your cheeks, I like your nose,
I like the way your lips disclose
The neat arrangement of your teeth
(Half above and half beneath)
 In rows.

I like your eyes, I like their fringes.
The way they focus on me gives me twinges.
Your upper arms drive me berserk.
I like the way your elbows work,
 On hinges.

I like your wrists, I like your glands,
I like the fingers on your hands.
I'd like to teach them how to count,
And certain things we might exchange,
Something familiar for something strange.
I'd like to give you just the right amount
    And get some change.

I like it when you tilt your cheek up.
I like the way you nod and hold a teacup.
I like your legs when you unwind them.
Even in trousers I don't mind them.
I like each softly-moulded kneecap.
I like the little crease behind them.
I'd always know, without a recap,
    Where to find them.

I like the sculpture of your ears.
I like the way your profile disappears
Whenever you decide to turn and face me.
I'd like to cross two hemispheres
    And have you chase me.
I'd like to smuggle you across frontiers
Or sail with you at night into Tangiers.
    I'd like you to embrace me.

I'd like to see you ironing your skirt
    And cancelling other dates.
I'd like to button up your shirt.
I like the way your chest inflates.
I'd like to soothe you when you're hurt
Or frightened senseless by invertebrates.

I'd like you even if you were malign
And had a yen for sudden homicide.
I'd let you put insecticide
    Into my wine.
I'd even like you if you were the Bride
    Of Frankenstein
Or something ghoulish out of Mamoulian's
    Jekyll and Hyde.
I'd even like you as my Julian
Of Norwich or Cathleen ni Houlihan.
    How melodramatic
If you were something muttering in attics
Like Mrs Rochester or a student of Boolean
    Mathematics.

You are the end of self-abuse.
You are the eternal feminine.
I'd like to find a good excuse
To call on you and find you in.
I'd like to put my hand beneath your chin,
    And see you grin.
I'd like to taste your Charlotte Russe,
I'd like to feel my lips upon your skin,
I'd like to make you reproduce.

I'd like you in my confidence.
I'd like to be your second look.
I'd like to let you try the French Defence
    And mate you with my rook.
I'd like to be your preference
    And hence
I'd like to be around when you unhook.
I'd like to be your only audience,
The final name in your appointment book,
    Your future tense.

JOHN FULLER

Come. And Be My Baby

The highway is full of big cars going nowhere fast
And folks is smoking anything that'll burn
Some people wrap their lives around a cocktail glass
And you sit wondering
where you're going to turn
I got it.
Come. And be my baby.

Some prophets say the world is gonna end tomorrow
But others say we've got a week or two
The paper is full of every kind of blooming horror
And you sit wondering
what you're gonna do.
I got it.
Come. And be my baby.

MAYA ANGELOU

The Orange

At lunchtime I bought a huge orange —
The size of it made us all laugh.
I peeled it and shared it with Robert and Dave —
They got quarters and I had a half.

And that orange, it made me so happy,
As ordinary things often do
Just lately. The shopping. A walk in the park.
This is peace and contentment. It's new.

The rest of the day was quite easy.
I did all the jobs on my list
And enjoyed them and had some time over.
I love you. I'm glad I exist.

WENDY COPE

⚘ Valentine ⚘

Not a red rose or a satin heart.

I give you an onion.
It is a moon wrapped in brown paper.
It promises light
like the careful undressing of love.

Here.
It will blind you with tears
like a lover.
It will make your reflection
a wobbling photo of grief.

I am trying to be truthful.

Not a cute card or a kissogram.

I give you an onion.
Its fierce kiss will stay on your lips,
possessive and faithful
as we are,
for as long as we are.

Take it.
Its platinum loops shrink to a wedding-ring,
if you like.
Lethal.
Its scent will cling to your fingers,
cling to your knife.

CAROL ANN DUFFY

Words, Wide Night

Somewhere, on the other side of this wide night
and the distance between us, I am thinking of you.
The room is turning slowly away from the moon.

This is pleasurable. Or shall I cross that out and say
it is sad? In one of the tenses I singing
an impossible song of desire that you cannot hear.

La lala la. See? I close my eyes and imagine
the dark hills I would have to cross
to reach you. For I am in love with you and this

is what it is like or what it is like in words.

CAROL ANN DUFFY

If Passionate

'Where true Love burns,
Desire is Love's pure flame'

SAMUEL TAYLOR COLERIDGE, FROM 'DESIRE'

Doing, a filthy pleasure is, and short

Doing, a filthy pleasure is, and short;
And done, we straight repent us of the sport:
Let us not then rush blindly on unto it,
Like lustful beasts, that only know to do it:
For lust will languish, and that heat decay.
But thus, thus, keeping endless holiday,
Let us together closely lie and kiss,
There is no labour, nor no shame in this;
This hath pleased, doth please, and long will please; never
Can this decay, but is beginning ever.

PETRONIUS
(TRANSLATED FROM THE LATIN BY BEN JONSON)

The Passionate Shepherd to His Love

Come live with me and be my love,
And we will all the pleasures prove
That valleys, groves, hills and fields,
Woods, or steepy mountain yields.

And we will sit upon the rocks,
Seeing the shepherds feed their flocks
By shallow rivers, to whose falls
Melodious birds sing madrigals.

And I will make thee beds of roses,
And a thousand fragrant posies,
A cap of flowers, and a kirtle,
Embroidered all with leaves of myrtle.

A gown made of the finest wool
Which from our pretty lambs we pull,
Fair linèd slippers for the cold,
With buckles of the purest gold.

A belt of straw and ivy-buds,
With coral clasps and amber studs,
And if these pleasures may thee move,
Come live with me, and be my love.

The shepherd swains shall dance and sing
For thy delight each May morning.
If these delights thy mind may move,
Then live with me, and be my love.

CHRISTOPHER MARLOWE

The Good Morrow

I wonder, by my troth, what thou and I
Did, till we loved? were we not weaned till then?
But sucked on country pleasures, childishly?
Or snorted we in the seven sleepers' den?
'Twas so; but this, all pleasures fancies be.
If ever any beauty I did see,
Which I desired, and got, 'twas but a dream of thee.

And now good morrow to our waking souls,
Which watch not one another out of fear;
For love, all love of other sights controls,
And makes one little room, an everywhere.
Let sea-discoverers to new worlds have gone,
Let maps to others, worlds on worlds have shown,
Let us possess one world, each hath one, and is one.

My face in thine eye, thine in mine appears,
And true plain hearts do in the faces rest;
Where can we find two better hemispheres,
Without sharp north, without declining west?
Whatever dies, was not mixed equally;
If our two loves be one, or, thou and I
Love so alike, that none do slacken, none can die.

JOHN DONNE

41

To His Coy Mistress

Had we but world enough, and time,
This coyness, Lady, were no crime.
We would sit down, and think which way
To walk, and pass our long love's day;
Thou by the Indian Ganges' side
Shouldst rubies find: I by the tide
Of Humber would complain. I would
Love you ten years before the flood:
And you should, if you please, refuse
Till the conversion of the Jews.
My vegetable love should grow
Vaster than empires, and more slow.
An hundred years should go to praise
Thine eyes, and on thy forehead gaze.
Two hundred to adore each breast:
But thirty thousand to the rest.
An age at least to every part,
And the last age should show your heart:
For, Lady, you deserve this state;
Nor would I love at lower rate.
    But at my back I always hear
Time's wingèd chariot hurrying near:
And yonder all before us lie
Deserts of vast eternity.
Thy beauty shall no more be found;
Nor, in thy marble vault, shall sound
My echoing song: then worms shall try
That long-preserved virginity:
And your quaint honour turn to dust;
And into ashes all my lust.
The grave's a fine and private place,
But none I think do there embrace.
    Now, therefore, while the youthful hue
Sits on thy skin like morning dew,
And while thy willing soul transpires
At every pore with instant fires,
Now let us sport us while we may;

And now, like amorous birds of prey,
Rather at once our time devour,
Than languish in his slow-chapped power.
Let us roll all our strength, and all
Our sweetness, up into one ball:
And tear our pleasures with rough strife,
Thorough the iron gates of life.
Thus, though we cannot make our sun
Stand still, yet we will make him run.

ANDREW MARVELL

Upon Julia's Clothes

When as in silks my Julia goes,
Then, then (methinks) how sweetly flows
That liquefaction of her clothes.

Next, when I cast mine eyes and see
That brave Vibration each way free;
O how that glittering taketh me!

ROBERT HERRICK

A letter from Napoleon Bonaparte to Joséphine de Beauharnais

SENT FROM VERONA, 13 NOVEMBER 1796

I do not love thee any more; on the contrary, I detest thee. Thou art horrid, very awkward, very stupid, a very Cinderella. Thou dost not write me at all, thou dost not love thy husband; thou knowest the pleasure that thy letters afford him, and thou dost not write him six lines of even haphazard scribble.

What do you do then all day, Madame? What matter of such importance is it that takes up your time from writing to your very good lover? What affection stifles and pushes on one side the love, the tender and constant love, which you have promised him? Who can be this marvellous, this new lover who absorbs all your instants, tyrannises your entire days, and prevents you from being solicitous about your husband? Joséphine, beware, one fine night the doors will break open and I will be there.

In truth, I am anxious, my good *amie*, at not receiving your news; write me quickly four pages, and say those amiable things which fill my heart with sentiment and pleasure.

I hope before long to press you in my arms and shall shower on you a million burning kisses as under the equator.

Bonaparte

Napoleon proposed to Joséphine, a widow six years his senior with whom he had been having a passionate affair, in January 1796. The marriage was not well-received by his family, who felt he could have chosen a more appropriate wife. Two days after their marriage, Napoleon left to lead the army in Italy, the separation that produced these letters. Alone and isolated in Paris, Joséphine began an affair, news of which reached Napoleon. Napoleon too began to have affairs, and divorced Joséphine in 1810, probably because she could not give him children. He remarried, but the two remained on good terms until her death. Napoleon saw to it that she retained the title of Empress, and told her that she could 'ever hold me as her best and dearest friend'.

Lochinvar

O, young Lochinvar is come out of the west,
Through all the wide Border his steed was the best;
And save his good broadsword he weapons had none,
He rode all unarm'd, and he rode all alone.
So faithful in love, and so dauntless in war,
There never was knight like the young Lochinvar.

He stayed not for brake, and he stopped not for stone,
He swam the Eske river where ford there was none;
But ere he alighted at Netherby gate,
The bride had consented, the gallant came late:
For a laggard in love, and a dastard in war,
Was to wed the fair Ellen of brave Lochinvar.

So boldly he entered the Netherby Hall,
Among bride's-men, and kinsmen, and brothers and all:
Then spoke the bride's father, his hand on his sword,
(For the poor craven bridegroom said never a word,)
'O come ye in peace here, or come ye in war,
Or to dance at our bridal, young Lord Lochinvar?'

'I long woo'd your daughter, my suit you denied; –
Love swells like the Solway, but ebbs like its tide –
And now I am come, with this lost love of mine,
To lead but one measure, drink one cup of wine.
There are maidens in Scotland more lovely by far,
That would gladly be bride to the young Lochinvar.'

The bride kiss'd the goblet: the knight took it up,
He quaffed off the wine, and he threw down the cup.
She looked down to blush, and she looked up to sigh,
With a smile on her lips and a tear in her eye.
He took her soft hand, ere her mother could bar, –
'Now tread we a measure!' said young Lochinvar.

So stately his form, and so lovely her face,
That never a hall such a galliard did grace;
While her mother did fret, and her father did fume
And the bridegroom stood dangling his bonnet and plume;
And the bride-maidens whispered, "Twere better by far
To have match'd our fair cousin with young Lochinvar.'

One touch to her hand, and one word in her ear,
When they reached the hall-door, and the charger stood near;
So light to the croupe the fair lady he swung,
So light to the saddle before her he sprung!
'She is won! we are gone, over bank, bush, and scaur;
They'll have fleet steeds that follow,' quoth young Lochinvar.

There was mounting 'mong Graemes of the Netherby clan;
Forsters, Fenwicks, and Musgraves, they rode and they ran:
There was racing and chasing on Cannobie Lee,
But the lost bride of Netherby ne'er did they see.
So daring in love, and so dauntless in war,
Have ye e'er heard of gallant like young Lochinvar?

SIR WALTER SCOTT

⫍ Desire ⫎

Where true Love burns, Desire is Love's pure flame;
It is the reflex of our earthly frame,
That takes its meaning from the nobler part,
And but translates the language of the heart.

SAMUEL TAYLOR COLERIDGE

Love's Philosophy

The fountains mingle with the river
    And the rivers with the ocean,
The winds of heaven mix forever
    With a sweet emotion;
Nothing in the world is single;
    All things by a law divine
In another's being mingle:
    Why not I with thine?

See the mountains kiss high heaven,
    And the waves clasp one another;
No sister flower could be forgiven
    If it disdained its brother;
And the sunlight clasps the earth,
    And the moonbeams kiss the sea:
What are all these kissings worth,
    If thou kiss not me?

PERCY BYSSHE SHELLEY

To Fanny

I cry your mercy, pity, love – ay, love!
    Merciful love that tantalizes not,
One-thoughted, never-wandering, guileless love,
    Unmasked, and being seen – without a blot!
O! let me have thee whole, – all, all, be mine!
    That shape, that fairness, that sweet minor zest
Of love, your kiss – those hands, those eyes divine,
    That warm, white, lucent, million-pleasured breast –
Yourself – your soul – in pity give me all,
    Withhold no atom's atom or I die,
Or living on perhaps, your wretched thrall,
    Forget, in the mist of idle misery,
Life's purposes – the palate of my mind
Losing its gust, and my ambition blind!

JOHN KEATS

Now sleeps the crimson petal

Now sleeps the crimson petal, now the white;
Nor waves the cypress in the palace walk;
Nor winks the gold fin in the porphyry font:
The fire-fly wakens: waken thou with me.

Now droops the milkwhite peacock like a ghost,
And like a ghost she glimmers on to me.

Now lies the Earth all Danaë to the stars,
And all thy heart lies open unto me.

Now slides the silent meteor on, and leaves
A shining furrow, as thy thoughts in me.

Now folds the lily all her sweetness up,
And slips into the bosom of the lake:
So fold thyself, my dearest, thou, and slip
Into my bosom and be lost in me.

ALFRED, LORD TENNYSON, FROM *THE PRINCESS*

❧ Now ❧

Out of your whole life give but a moment!
All of your life that has gone before,
All to come after it, – so you ignore,
So you make perfect the present, – condense,
In a rapture of rage, for perfection's endowment,
Thought and feeling and soul and sense –
Merged in a moment which gives me at last
You around me for once, you beneath me, above me –
Me – sure that despite of time future, time past, –
This tick of life-time's one moment you love me!
How long such suspension may linger? Ah, Sweet –
The moment eternal – just that and no more –
When ecstasy's utmost we clutch at the core
While cheeks burn, arms open, eyes shut, and lips meet!

ROBERT BROWNING

Meeting at Night

The grey sea and the long black land;
And the yellow half-moon large and low;
And the startled little waves that leap
In fiery ringlets from their sleep,
As I gain the cove with pushing prow,
And quench its speed i' the slushy sand.

Then a mile of warm sea-scented beach;
Three fields to cross till a farm appears;
A tap at the pane, the quick sharp scratch
And blue spurt of a lighted match,
And a voice less loud, thro' its joys and fears,
Than the two hearts beating each to each!

ROBERT BROWNING

↗ from Wuthering Heights ↙

'I think that's the worst motive you've given yet for being the wife of young Linton.'

'It is not,' retorted she; 'it is the best! The others were the satisfaction of my whims: and for Edgar's sake, too, to satisfy him. This is for the sake of one who comprehends in his person my feelings to Edgar and myself. I cannot express it; but surely you and everybody have a notion that there is or should be an existence of yours beyond you. What were the use of my creation, if I were entirely contained here? My great miseries in this world have been Heathcliff's miseries, and I watched and felt each from the beginning: my great thought in living is himself. If all else perished, and he remained, I should still continue to be; and if all else remained, and he were annihilated, the universe would turn to a mighty stranger: I should not seem a part of it.—My love for Linton is like the foliage in the woods: time will change it, I'm well aware, as winter changes the trees. My love for Heathcliff resembles the eternal rocks beneath: a source of little visible delight, but necessary. Nelly, I am Heathcliff! He's always, always in my mind: not as a pleasure, any more than I am always a pleasure to myself, but as my own being.'

EMILY BRONTË

To a Stranger

Passing stranger! you do not know how longingly I look upon you,
You must be he I was seeking, or she I was seeking, (it comes to me as of a
dream,)
I have somewhere surely lived a life of joy with you,
All is recall'd as we flit by each other, fluid, affectionate, chaste, matured,
You grew up with me, were a boy with me or a girl with me,
I ate with you and slept with you, your body has become not yours only nor
left my body mine only,
You give me the pleasure of your eyes, face, flesh, as we pass, you take of
my beard, breast, hands, in return,
I am not to speak to you, I am to think of you when I sit alone or wake at
night alone,
I am to wait, I do not doubt I am to meet you again,
I am to see to it that I do not lose you.

WALT WHITMAN

A Glimpse

A glimpse through an interstice caught,
Of a crowd of workmen and drivers in a bar-room around the stove late of a
    winter night, and I unremark'd seated in a corner,
Of a youth who loves me and whom I love, silently approaching and seating
    himself near, that he may hold me by the hand,
A long while amid the noises of coming and going, of drinking and oath and
    smutty jest,
There we two, content, happy in being together, speaking little, perhaps not
    a word.

WALT WHITMAN

Her breast is fit for pearls

Her breast is fit for pearls,
But I was not a 'Diver.'
Her brow is fit for thrones —
But I have not a crest.
Her heart is fit for home —
I — a sparrow — build there
Sweet of twigs and twine
My perennial nest.

EMILY DICKINSON

Wild nights - Wild nights!

Wild nights -Wild nights!
Were I with thee
Wild nights should be
Our luxury!

Futile - the winds -
To a Heart in port -
Done with the Compass -
Done with the Chart!

Rowing in Eden -
Ah - the Sea!
Might I but moor - tonight -
In thee!

EMILY DICKINSON

Love and Sleep

Lying asleep between the strokes of night
   I saw my love lean over my sad bed,
   Pale as the duskiest lily's leaf or head,
Smooth-skinned and dark, with bare throat made to bite,
Too wan for blushing and too warm for white,
   But perfect-coloured without white or red.
   And her lips opened amorously, and said –
I wist not what, saving one word – Delight.

And all her face was honey to my mouth,
   And all her body pasture to mine eyes;
      The long lithe arms and hotter hands than fire,
The quivering flanks, hair smelling of the south,
   The bright light feet, the splendid supple thighs
      And glittering eyelids of my soul's desire.

ALGERNON CHARLES SWINBURNE

Leda and the Swan

A sudden blow: the great wings beating still
Above the staggering girl, her thighs caressed
By the dark webs, her nape caught in his bill,
He holds her helpless breast upon his breast.

How can those terrified vague fingers push
The feathered glory from her loosening thighs?
And how can body, laid in that white rush,
But feel the strange heart beating where it lies?

A shudder in the loins engenders there
The broken wall, the burning roof and tower
And Agamemnon dead.
                    Being so caught up,
So mastered by the brute blood of the air,
Did she put on his knowledge with his power
Before the indifferent beak could let her drop?

W.B. YEATS

∽ A Decade ∾

When you came, you were like red wine and honey,
And the taste of you burnt my mouth with its sweetness.
Now you are like morning bread,
Smooth and pleasant.
I hardly taste you at all for I know your savour,
But I am completely nourished.

AMY LOWELL

A letter from Virginia Woolf to Vita Sackville-West

52 TAVISTOCK SQUARE
SUNDAY [7 OCTOBER]

Dearest Creature,

It was a very very nice letter you wrote by the light of the stars at midnight. Always write then, for your heart requires moonlight to deliquesce it. And mine is fried in gaslight, as it is only nine o'clock and I must go to bed at eleven. And so I shant say anything: not a word of the balm to my anguish - for I am always anguished - that you were to me. How I watched you! How I felt - now what was it like? Well, somewhere I have seen a little ball kept bubbling up and down on the spray of a fountain: the fountain is you; the ball me. It is a sensation I get only from you. It is physically stimulating, restful at the same time...

Berg

Virginia Woolf (née Stephen) and Vita Sackville-West's affair of the early 1920s was, in fact, disturbed very little by Sackville-West's husband, Harold Nicolson. Theirs was an open marriage, during which they both had same-sex extramarital affairs, and frequently shared news of them with each other. After Vita's relationship with Virginia ended, Virginia went on to marry Leonard Woolf. The two remained friends, however, and twelve years after their affair, Sackville-West wrote of still remembering ' how the ceilings of Long Barn once swayed above us'.

from Orlando

A melon, an emerald, a fox in the snow — so he raved, so he stared. When the boy, for alas, a boy it must be — no woman could skate with such speed and vigour — swept almost on tiptoe past him, Orlando was ready to tear his hair with vexation that the person was of his own sex, and thus all embraces were out of the question. But the skater came closer. Legs, hands, carriage, were a boy's, but no boy ever had a mouth like that; no boy had those breasts; no boy had eyes which looked as if they had been fished from the bottom of the sea. Finally, coming to a stop and sweeping a curtsey with the utmost grace to the King, who was shuffling past on the arm of some Lord-in-waiting, the unknown skater came to a standstill. She was not a handsbreadth off. She was a woman. Orlando stared; trembled; turned hot; turned cold; longed to hurl himself through the summer air; to crush acorns beneath his feet; to toss his arm with the beech trees and the oaks. As it was, he drew his lips up over his small white teeth; opened them perhaps half an inch as if to bite; shut them as if he had bitten.

VIRGINIA WOOLF

New Year's Eve

There are only two things now,
The great black night scooped out
And this fireglow.

This fireglow, the core,
And we the two ripe pips
That are held in store.

Listen, the darkness rings
As it circulates round our fire.
Take off your things.

Your shoulders, your bruised throat!
Your breasts, your nakedness!
This fiery coat!

As the darkness flickers and dips,
As the firelight falls and leaps
From your feet to your lips!

D.H. LAWRENCE

A letter from Katherine Mansfield to John Middleton Murry

28 MARCH 1915

Jack, I shan't hide what I feel today. I woke up with you in my breast and on my lips. Jack, I love you terribly today. The whole world is gone. It is only you. I walk about, dress, eat, write – but all the time I am *breathing* you. Time and again I have been on the point of telegraphing you that I am coming home as soon as Kay sends my money. It is still possible that I shall.

> *Jack, Jack, I want to come back,*
> *And hear the little ducks go*
> *Quack! Quack! Quack!*

Life is too short for our love even though we stayed together every moment of all the years. I cannot think of you – our life – our darling life – you, my treasure – everything about you.

No, no, no. Take me quickly into your arms. Tig is a tired girl and she is crying. I want you, I want you. Without you life is nothing.

Your woman

Tig

Mansfield and her husband John Middleton Murry first met when Murry rejected a story that Mansfield had submitted to his literary magazine. Mansfield's divorce from her first husband had still not been finalised, and their relationship, though passionate, was troubled by debts, affairs and bereavements. Though they married in 1918, they continued to repeatedly separate and reunite, and Mansfield's slow decline from tuberculosis placed further strain on their marriage. Mansfield died in 1923, after suffering a fatal haemorrhage when she ran up a flight of stairs to demonstrate to Murry how healthy she was. After her death, he remarried, but his new wife Violet bore an uncanny resemblance to Katherine. He proposed to her with Katherine's ring, lived in a house filled with Katherine's furniture and named their first daughter Katherine. Violet too died of tuberculosis in 1931, having been diagnosed by the same doctor who had attended to Katherine.

from My Diary, July 1914

Leaves
    Murmuring by myriads in the shimmering trees.
Lives
    Wakening with wonder in the Pyrenees.
Birds
    Cheerily chirping in the early day.
Bards
    Singing of summer, scything through the hay.
Bees
    Shaking the heavy dews from bloom and frond.
Boys
    Bursting the surface of the ebony pond.
Flashes
    Of swimmers carving through the sparkling cold.
Fleshes
    Gleaming with wetness to the morning gold.
A mead
    Bordered about with warbling water brooks.
A maid
    Laughing the love-laugh with me; proud of looks.
The heat
    Throbbing between the upland and the peak.
Her heart
    Quivering with passion to my pressèd cheek.
Braiding
    Of floating flames across the mountain brow.
Brooding
    Of stillness; and a sighing of the bough.
Stirs
    Of leaflets in the gloom; soft petal-showers;
Stars
    Expanding with the starr'd nocturnal flowers.

WILFRED OWEN

On the Marriage of a Virgin

Waking alone in a multitude of loves when morning's light
Surprised in the opening of her nightlong eyes
His golden yesterday asleep upon the iris
And this day's sun leapt up the sky out of her thighs
Was miraculous virginity old as loaves and fishes,
Though the moment of a miracle is unending lightning
And the shipyards of Galilee's footprints hide a navy of doves.

No longer will the vibrations of the sun desire on
Her deepsea pillow where once she married alone,
Her heart all ears and eyes, lips catching the avalanche
Of the golden ghost who ringed with his streams her mercury bone,
Who under the lids of her windows hoisted his golden luggage,
For a man sleeps where fire leapt down and she learns through his arm
That other sun, the jealous coursing of the unrivalled blood.

DYLAN THOMAS

Bride and Groom Lie
Hidden for Three Days

She gives him his eyes, she found them
Among some rubble, among some beetles

He gives her her skin
He just seemed to pull it down out of the air and lay it over her
She weeps with fearfulness and astonishment

She has found his hands for him, and fitted them freshly at the wrists
They are amazed at themselves, they go feeling all over her

He has assembled her spine, he cleaned each piece carefully
And sets them in perfect order
A superhuman puzzle but he is inspired
She leans back twisting this way and that, using it and laughing
Incredulous

Now she has brought his feet, she is connecting them
So that his whole body lights up
And he has fashioned her new hips
With all fittings complete and with newly wound coils, all shiningly oiled
He is polishing every part, he himself can hardly believe it

They keep taking each other to the sun, they find they can easily
To test each new thing at each new step

And now she smoothes over him the plates of his skull
So that the joints are invisible

And now he connects her throat, her breasts and the pit of her stomach
With a single wire

She gives him his teeth, tying their roots to the centrepin of his body

He sets the little circlets on her fingertips

She stitches his body here and there with steely purple silk

He oils the delicate cogs of her mouth

She inlays with deep-cut scrolls the nape of his neck

He sinks into place the inside of her thighs

So, gasping with joy, with cries of wonderment
Like two gods of mud
Sprawling in the dirt, but with infinite care

They bring each other to perfection.

TED HUGHES

The Bed

The pulsing stops where time has been,
The garden is snow-bound,
The branches weighed down and the paths filled in,
Drifts quilt the ground.

We lie soft-caught, still now it's done,
Loose-twined across the bed
Like wrestling statues; but it still goes on
Inside my head.

THOM GUNN

✒ Coupling ✑

On the wall above the bedside lamp
a large crane-fly is jump-starting
a smaller crane-fly — or vice versa.
They do it tail to tail, like Volkswagens:
their engines must be in their rears.

It looks easy enough. Let's try it.

FLEUR ADCOCK

Trysts

meet me
where the sun goes down
meet me
in the cave, under the battleground
meet me
on the broken branch
meet me
in the shade, below the avalanche
meet me
under the witch's spell
meet me
tonight, in the wishing well
meet me
on the famine lawn
meet me
in the eye of the firestorm
meet me
in your best shoes
and your favourite dress
meet me
on your own, in the wilderness
meet me
as my lover, as my only friend
meet me
on the river bed

ROBIN ROBERTSON

'And at home by the fire, whenever
you look up there I shall be— and
whenever I look up, there will be you.'

THOMAS HARDY, FROM *FAR FROM THE MADDING CROWD*

The Bargain

My true love hath my heart, and I have his,
    By just exchange one for the other given.
I hold his dear, and mine he cannot miss,
    There never was a bargain better driven.
His heart in me keeps me and him in one,
    My heart in him his thoughts and senses guides;
He loves my heart for once it was his own,
    I cherish his because in me it bides.
His heart his wound receivèd from my sight;
    My heart was wounded with his wounded heart;
For as from me on him his hurt did light,
    So still methought in me his hurt did smart:
        Both equal hurt, in this change sought our bliss:
        My true love hath my heart and I have his.

SIR PHILIP SIDNEY,
FROM *THE COUNTESS OF PEMBROKE'S ARCADIA*

Sonnet 116

(LET ME NOT TO THE MARRIAGE OF TRUE MINDS)

Let me not to the marriage of true minds
Admit impediments; love is not love
Which alters when it alteration finds,
Or bends with the remover to remove.
O no, it is an ever-fixed mark
That looks on tempests and is never shaken;
It is the star to every wand'ring bark,
Whose worth's unknown, although his height be taken.
Love's not time's fool, though rosy lips and cheeks
Within his bending sickle's compass come;
Love alters not with his brief hours and weeks,
But bears it out even to the edge of doom.
　If this be error and upon me proved,
　I never writ, nor no man ever loved.

WILLIAM SHAKESPEARE

Lovers' Infiniteness

If yet I have not all thy love,
Dear, I shall never have it all;
I cannot breathe one other sigh, to move,
Nor can entreat one other tear to fall.
And all my treasure, which should purchase thee,
Sighs, tears, and oaths, and letters I have spent;
Yet no more can be due to me,
Than at the bargain made was meant.
If then thy gift of love were partial,
That some to me, some should to others fall,
    Dear, I shall never have thee all.

Or if then thou gavest me all,
All was but all, which thou hadst then;
But if in thy heart, since, there be or shall
New love created be, by other men,
Which have their stocks entire, and can in tears,
In sighs, in oaths, and letters, outbid me,
This new love may beget new fears,
For this love was not vow'd by thee.
And yet it was, thy gift being general,
The ground, thy heart, is mine; what ever shall
    Grow there, dear, I should have it all.

Yet I would not have all yet.
He that hath all can have no more;
And since my love doth every day admit
New growth, thou shouldst have new rewards in store.
Thou canst not every day give me thy heart.
If thou canst give it, then thou never gavest it:
Love's riddles are, that though thy heart depart,
It stays at home, and thou with losing savest it:
But we will have a way more liberal,
Than changing hearts, to join them; so we shall
    Be one, and one another's all.

JOHN DONNE

77

from The Song of Solomon

THE KING JAMES BIBLE

Set me as a seal upon thine heart, as a seal upon thine arm: for love is strong as death; jealousy is cruel as the grave: the coals thereof are coals of fire, which hath a most vehement flame. Many waters cannot quench love, neither can the floods drown it: if a man would give all the substance of his house for love, it would utterly be contemned.

I Corinthians 13

THE KING JAMES BIBLE

Though I speak with the tongues of men and of angels, and have not love, I am become as sounding brass, or a tinkling cymbal. And though I have the gift of prophecy, and understand all mysteries, and all knowledge; and though I have all faith, so that I could remove mountains, and I have not love, I am nothing. And though I bestow all my goods to feed the poor, and though I give my body to be burned, and have not love, it profiteth me nothing.

Love suffereth, and is kind; love envieth not; love vaunteth not itself, is not puffed up, Doth not behave itself unseemly, seeketh not her own, is not easily provoked, thinketh no evil; Rejoiceth not in iniquity, but rejoiceth in the truth; Beareth all things, believeth all things, hopeth all things, endureth all things.

Love never faileth: but whether there be prophecies, they shall fail; whether there be tongues, they shall cease; whether there be knowledge, it shall vanish away. For we know in part, and we prophesy in part. But when that which is perfect is come, then that which is in part shall be done away. When I was a child, I spake as a child, I understood as a child, I thought as a child: but when I became a man, I put away childish things. For now we see through a glass, darkly; but then face to face: now I know in part; but then shall I know even as also I am known. And now abideth faith, hope, love, these three; but the greatest of these is love.

To My Dear and Loving Husband

If ever two were one, then surely we.
If ever man were loved by wife, then thee.
If ever wife was happy in a man,
Compare with me, ye women, if you can.
I prize thy love more than whole mines of gold,
Or all the riches that the east doth hold.
My love is such that rivers cannot quench,
Nor ought but love from thee give recompense.
Thy love is such I can no way repay;
The heavens reward thee manifold, I pray.
Then while we live, in love let's so persever,
That when we live no more we may live ever.

ANNE BRADSTREET

A letter from Wolfgang Amadeus Mozart to Constanze Mozart

SENT FROM DRESDEN, 16 APRIL 1789

Dear little wife, I have a number of requests to make. I beg you

(1) not to be melancholy,

(2) to take care of your health and to beware of the spring breezes,

(3) not to go out walking alone – and preferably not to go out walking at all,

(4) to feel absolutely assured of my love. Up to the present I have not written a single letter to you without placing your dear portrait before me.

(5) I beg in your conduct not only to be careful of your honour and mine, but also to consider appearances. Do not be angry with me for asking this. You ought to love me even more for thus valuing our honour.

(6) and lastly I beg you to send me more details in your letters. I should very much like to know whether our brother-in-law Hofer came to see us the day after my departure? Whether he comes very often, as he promised me he would? Whether the Langes come sometimes? Whether progress is being made with the portrait? What sort of life you are leading? All these things are naturally of great interest to me.

W. A. Mozart

Wolfgang Amadeus Mozart met Constanze Weber in 1781, when she was just 19. They had a tempestuous relationship which was vehemently disapproved of by Mozart's father. Mozart, regarded as one of the greatest and most influential composers of the Classical period, wrote some of his most famous soprano solos for Constanze, who was a talented singer and musician herself. They briefly broke up when Mozart became jealous after Constanze allowed another man to measure her calves in a parlour game. The two reunited and courted scandal by moving in together before marriage, eventually forcing Mozart's father to give his permission to the union. They remained together until Mozart's death and had six children, four of whom died before their first birthday.

A Red, Red Rose

My luve is like a red, red rose,
　　That's newly sprung in June:
My luve is like the melodie,
　　That's sweetly play'd in tune.
As fair art thou, my bonnie lass,
　　So deep in luve am I,
And I will luve thee still, my dear,
　　Till a' the seas gang dry.

Till a' the seas gang dry, my dear,
　　And the rocks melt wi' the sun!
And I will luve thee still, my dear,
　　While the sands o' life shall run.
And fare-thee-weel, my only luve,
　　And fare-thee-weel, a while!
And I will come again, my luve,
Tho' it were ten thousand mile.

ROBERT BURNS

⦿ Sonnet 14 ⦿

(IF THOU MUST LOVE ME)

If thou must love me, let it be for nought
Except for love's sake only. Do not say
'I love her for her smile... her look... her way
Of speaking gently,... for a trick of thought
That falls in well with mine, and certes brought
A sense of pleasant ease on such a day' -
For these things in themselves, Belovèd, may
Be changed, or change for thee, - and love, so wrought,
May be unwrought so. Neither love me for
Thine own dear pity's wiping my cheeks dry, -
A creature might forget to weep, who bore
Thy comfort long, and lose thy love thereby!
But love me for love's sake, that evermore
Thou may'st love on, through love's eternity.

ELIZABETH BARRETT BROWNING

⚘ Sonnet 43 ⚘

(HOW DO I LOVE THEE?)

How do I love thee? Let me count the ways.
I love thee to the depth and breadth and height
My soul can reach, when feeling out of sight
For the ends of Being and Ideal Grace.
I love thee to the level of every day's
Most quiet need, by sun and candlelight.
I love thee freely, as men strive for Right;
I love thee purely, as they turn from Praise.
I love thee with a passion, put to use
In my old griefs, and with my childhood's faith.
I love thee with a love I seemed to lose
With my lost saints, – I love thee with the breath,
Smiles, tears, of all my life! – and, if God choose,
I shall but love thee better after death.

ELIZABETH BARRETT BROWNING

The Owl and the Pussy-cat

The Owl and the Pussy-cat went to sea
    In a beautiful pea-green boat,
They took some honey, and plenty of money,
    Wrapped up in a five-pound note.
The Owl looked up to the stars above,
    And sang to a small guitar,
'O lovely Pussy! O Pussy, my love,
    What a beautiful Pussy you are,
      You are,
      You are!
What a beautiful Pussy you are!'

Pussy said to the Owl, 'You elegant fowl!
    How charmingly sweet you sing!
O let us be married! too long we have tarried:
    But what shall we do for a ring?'
They sailed away, for a year and a day,
    To the land where the Bong-tree grows
And there in a wood a Piggy-wig stood
    With a ring at the end of his nose,
      His nose,
      His nose,
  With a ring at the end of his nose.

'Dear Pig, are you willing to sell for one shilling
    Your ring?' Said the Piggy, 'I will.'
So they took it away, and were married next day
    By the Turkey who lives on the hill.
They dined on mince, and slices of quince,
    Which they ate with a runcible spoon;
And hand in hand, on the edge of the sand,
    They danced by the light of the moon,
      The moon,
      The moon,
They danced by the light of the moon.

EDWARD LEAR

Dover Beach

The sea is calm to-night.
The tide is full, the moon lies fair
Upon the straits; on the French coast the light
Gleams and is gone; the cliffs of England stand,
Glimmering and vast, out in the tranquil bay.
Come to the window, sweet is the night-air!
Only, from the long line of spray
Where the sea meets the moon-blanched land,
Listen! you hear the grating roar
Of pebbles which the waves draw back, and fling,
At their return, up the high strand,
Begin, and cease, and then again begin,
With tremulous cadence slow, and bring
The eternal note of sadness in.

Sophocles long ago
Heard it on the Ægaean, and it brought
Into his mind the turbid ebb and flow
Of human misery; we
Find also in the sound a thought,
Hearing it by this distant northern sea.

The Sea of Faith
Was once, too, at the full, and round earth's shore
Lay like the folds of a bright girdle furled.
But now I only hear
Its melancholy, long, withdrawing roar,
Retreating, to the breath
Of the night-wind, down the vast edges drear
And naked shingles of the world.

Ah, love, let us be true
To one another! for the world, which seems
To lie before us like a land of dreams,
So various, so beautiful, so new,
Hath really neither joy, nor love, nor light,
Nor certitude, nor peace, nor help for pain;
And we are here as on a darkling plain
Swept with confused alarms of struggle and flight,
Where ignorant armies clash by night.

MATTHEW ARNOLD

❧ A Marriage ❧

A marriage . . . makes of two fractional lives a whole; it gives two purposeless lives a work, and doubles the strength of each to perform it; it gives to two questioning natures a reason for living, and something to live for; it will give new gladness to the sunshine, a new fragrance to the flowers, a new beauty to the earth, and a new mystery to life.

MARK TWAIN

He Wishes for the Cloths of Heaven

Had I the heavens' embroidered cloths,
Enwrought with golden and silver light,
The blue and the dim and the dark cloths
Of night and light and the half-light,
I would spread the cloths under your feet:
But I, being poor, have only my dreams;
I have spread my dreams under your feet;
Tread softly because you tread on my dreams.

W.B. YEATS

Fidelity

Fidelity and love are two different things, like a flower and a gem.
And love, like a flower, will fade, will change into something else
or it would not be flowery.

O flowers they fade because they are moving swiftly; a little torrent of life
leaps up to the summit of the stem, gleams, turns over round the bend
of the parabola of curved flight,
sinks, and is gone, like a comet curving into the invisible.

O flowers they are all the time travelling
like comets, and they come into our ken
for a day, for two days, and withdraw, slowly vanish again.

And we, we must take them on the wing, and let them go.
Embalmed flowers are not flowers, immortelles are not flowers;
flowers are just a motion, a swift motion, a coloured gesture;
that is their loveliness. And that is love.

But a gem is different. It lasts so much longer than we do
so much much much longer
that it seems to last forever.
Yet we know it is flowing away
as flowers are, and we are, only slower.
The wonderful slow flowing of the sapphire!

All flows, and every flow is related to every other flow.
Flowers and sapphires and us, diversely streaming.
In the old days, when sapphires were breathed upon and brought forth
during the wild orgasms of chaos
time was much slower, when the rocks came forth.
It took aeons to make a sapphire, aeons for it to pass away.

And a flower it takes a summer.

And man and woman are like the earth, that brings forth flowers
in summer, and love, but underneath is rock.
Older than flowers, older than ferns, older than foraminiferae
older than plasm altogether is the soul of a man underneath.

And when, throughout all the wild orgasms of love
slowly a gem forms, in the ancient, once-more-molten rocks
of two human hearts, two ancient rocks, a man's heart and a woman's,
that is the crystal of peace, the slow hard jewel of trust,
the sapphire of fidelity.
The gem of mutual peace emerging from the wild chaos of love.

D. H. LAWRENCE

On Marriage

Then Almitra spoke again and said, 'And what of Marriage, master?'
And he answered saying:
You were born together, and together you shall be for evermore.
You shall be together when the white wings of death scatter your days.
Aye, you shall be together even in the silent memory of God.
But let there be spaces in your togetherness,
And let the winds of the heavens dance between you.

Love one another, but make not a bond of love:
Let it rather be a moving sea between the shores of your souls.
Fill each other's cup but drink not from one cup.
Give one another of your bread but eat not from the same loaf.
Sing and dance together and be joyous, but let each one of you be alone,
Even as the strings of a lute are alone though they quiver with the same music.

Give your hearts, but not into each other's keeping.
For only the hand of Life can contain your hearts.
And stand together, yet not too near together:
For the pillars of the temple stand apart,
And the oak tree and the cypress grow not in each other's shadow.

KAHLIL GIBRAN

A Dedication To My Wife

To whom I owe the leaping delight
That quickens my senses in our wakingtime
And the rhythm that governs the repose of our sleepingtime,
　　The breathing in unison

Of lovers whose bodies smell of each other
Who think the same thoughts without need of speech
And babble the same speech without need of meaning.

No peevish winter wind shall chill
No sullen tropic sun shall wither
The roses in the rose-garden which is ours and ours only

But this dedication is for others to read:
These are private words addressed to you in public.

T.S. ELIOT

Camomile Tea

Outside the sky is light with stars;
There's a hollow roaring from the sea.
And, alas! for the little almond flowers,
The wind is shaking the almond tree.

How little I thought, a year ago,
In the horrible cottage upon the Lee
That he and I should be sitting so
And sipping a cup of camomile tea.

Light as feathers the witches fly,
The horn of the moon is plain to see;
By a firefly under a jonquil flower
A goblin toasts a bumble-bee.

We might be fifty, we might be five,
So snug, so compact, so wise are we!
Under the kitchen-table leg
My knee is pressing against his knee.

Our shutters are shut, the fire is low,
The tap is dripping peacefully;
The saucepan shadows on the wall
Are black and round and plain to see.

KATHERINE MANSFIELD

i carry your heart with me
(i carry it in

i carry your heart with me(i carry it in
my heart)i am never without it(anywhere
i go you go,my dear;and whatever is done
by only me is your doing,my darling)
                              i fear
no fate(for you are my fate,my sweet)i want
no world(for beautiful you are my world,my true)
and it's you are whatever a moon has always meant
and whatever a sun will always sing is you

here is the deepest secret nobody knows
(here is the root of the root and the bud of the bud
and the sky of the sky of a tree called life;which grows
higher than soul can hope or mind can hide)
and this is the wonder that's keeping the stars apart

i carry your heart(i carry it in my heart)

E. E. CUMMINGS

A letter from Zelda Sayre to F. Scott Fitzgerald

MARCH 1919

Sweetheart,

Please, please don't be so depressed-We'll be married soon, and then these lonesome nights will be over forever-and until we are, I am loving, loving every tiny minute of the day and night- Maybe you won't understand this, but sometimes when I miss you most, it's hardest to write-and you always know when I make myself-Just the ache of it all-and I can't tell you.

If we were together, you'd feel how strong it is-you're so sweet when you're melancholy. I love your sad tenderness-when I've hurt you-That's one of the reasons I could never be sorry for our quarrels-and they bothered you so-Those dear, dear little fusses, when I always tried so hard to make you kiss and forget-

Scott-there's nothing in all the world I want but you-and your precious love-All the materials things are nothing.

I'd just hate to live a sordid, colorless existence-because you'd soon love me less-and less-and I'd do anything-anything--to keep your heart for my own-I don't want to live-I want to love first, and live incidentally...

Don't-don't ever think of the things you can't give me-You've trusted me with the dearest heart of all-and it's so damn much more than anybody else in all the world has ever had-

How can you think deliberately of life without me-If you should die--O Darling--darling Scott--It'd be like going blind...I'd have no purpose in life-just a pretty--decoration.

Don't you think I was made for you? I feel like you had me ordered-and I was delivered to you--to be worn-I want you to wear me, like a watch-charm or a button hole bouquet-to the world.

And then, when we're alone, I want to help-to know that you can't do anything without me...

All my heart--

I love you

Zelda

Zelda Sayre married F. Scott Fitzgerald in 1920 and this union was to become one of the twentieth century's most legendary romances. They were both glamorous, hugely talented writers but they were to encounter a life of career highs and lows, and do battle with his alcoholism and her mental illness.

Scaffolding

Masons, when they start upon a building,
Are careful to test out the scaffolding;

Make sure that planks won't slip at busy points,
Secure all ladders, tighten bolted joints.

And yet all this comes down when the job's done
Showing off walls of sure and solid stone.

So if, my dear, there sometimes seem to be
Old bridges breaking between you and me

Never fear. We may let the scaffolds fall
Confident that we have built our wall.

SEAMUS HEANEY

Hinterhof

Stay near to me and I'll stay near to you —
As near as you are dear to me will do,
   Near as the rainbow to the rain,
   The west wind to the windowpane,
As fire to the hearth, as dawn to dew.

Stay true to me and I'll stay true to you —
As true as you are new to me will do,
   New as the rainbow in the spray,
   Utterly new in every way,
New in the way that what you say is true.

Stay near to me, stay true to me. I'll stay
As near, as true to you as heart could pray.
   Heart never hoped that one might be
   Half of the things you are to me —
The dawn, the fire, the rainbow and the day.

JAMES FENTON

Let me put it this way

Let me put it this way:
if you came to lay

your sleeping head
against my arm or sleeve,

and if my arm went dead,
or if I had to take my leave

at midnight, I should rather
cleave it from the joint or seam

than make a scene
or bring you round.

There,
how does that sound?

SIMON ARMITAGE

The Vows

We pledge to wake each morning face-to-face,
to shun the orders of the busy sun,
we promise to disturb each other's peace.

And we will, yes, gaze at the pining moon,
will pick out brine-blown glass-gems from the strand,
will read our future scratched onto a stone.

We both believe that silence turns to sand
and promise not to add to the unsaid,
we meet here as the raging sea meets land.

We want the risen life before we're dead,
our passion will be squandered more than spent,
we hereby swear to spend our days in bed.

We're naked, till we wear each other's scent
and recognise it quicker than our own.
You start and finish me, you're my extent.

MICHAEL SYMMONS ROBERTS

Wedding

From time to time our love is like a sail
and when the sail begins to alternate
from tack to tack, it's like a swallowtail
and when the swallow flies it's like a coat;
and if the coat is yours, it has a tear
like a wide mouth and when the mouth begins
to draw the wind, it's like a trumpeter
and when the trumpet blows, it blows like millions . . .
and this, my love, when millions come and go
beyond the need of us, is like a trick;
and when the trick begins, it's like a toe
tip-toeing on a rope, which is like luck;
and when the luck begins, it's like a wedding,
which is like love, which is like everything.

ALICE OSWALD

'Well, as my tutor, Old Bubbleface
used to say, "Make love and be merry,
for tomorrow you may catch some
disgusting skin disease."'

RICHARD CURTIS AND BEN ELTON, FROM *BLACKADDER*

from Much Ado About Nothing, Act 2 Scene 3

BENEDICK

...Love me!
why, it must be requited. I hear how I am censured:
they say I will bear myself proudly, if I perceive
the love come from her; they say too that she will
rather die than give any sign of affection. I did
never think to marry: I must not seem proud: happy
are they that hear their detractions and can put
them to mending. They say the lady is fair; 'tis a
truth, I can bear them witness; and virtuous; 'tis
so, I cannot reprove it; and wise, but for loving
me; by my troth, it is no addition to her wit, nor
no great argument of her folly, for I will be
horribly in love with her. I may chance have some
odd quirks and remnants of wit broken on me,
because I have railed so long against marriage: but
doth not the appetite alter? a man loves the meat
in his youth that he cannot endure in his age.
Shall quips and sentences and these paper bullets of
the brain awe a man from the career of his humour?
No, the world must be peopled. When I said I would
die a bachelor, I did not think I should live till I
were married.

WILLIAM SHAKESPEARE

The Author loving these homely meats specially, viz.: Cream, Pancakes, Buttered Pippin-pies (laugh, good people) and Tobacco; writ to that worthy and virtuous gentlewoman, whom he calleth Mistress, as followeth

If there were, oh! an Hellespont of cream
Between us, milk-white mistress, I would swim
To you, to show to both my love's extreme,
Leander-like, - yea! dive from brim to brim.
But met I with a buttered pippin-pie
Floating upon't, that I would make my boat
To waft me to you without jeopardy,
Though sea-sick I might be while it did float.
Yet if a storm should rise, by night or day,
Of sugar-snows and hail of caraways,
Then, if I found a pancake in my way,
It like a plank should bring me to your kays;
   Which having found, if they tobacco kept,
   The smoke should dry me well before I slept.

JOHN DAVIES OF HEREFORD

The Flea

Mark but this flea, and mark in this,
How little that which thou deny'st me is;
Me it sucked first, and now sucks thee,
And in this flea, our two bloods mingled be;
Confess it, this cannot be said
A sin, or shame, or loss of maidenhead,
　　Yet this enjoys before it woo,
　　And pamper'd swells with one blood made of two,
　　And this, alas, is more than we would do.

O stay, three lives in one flea spare,
Where we almost, nay more than married are.
This flea is you and I, and this
Our marriage bed, and marriage temple is;
Though parents grudge, and you, we'are met,
And cloister'd in these living walls of jet.
　　Though use make you apt to kill me,
　　Let not to that self-murder added be,
　　And sacrilege, three sins in killing three.

Cruel and sudden, hast thou since
Purpled thy nail, in blood of innocence?
In what could this flea guilty be,
Except in that drop which it suck'd from thee?
Yet thou triumph'st, and say'st that thou
Find'st not thyself, nor me the weaker now;
　　'Tis true, then learn how false, fears be;
　　Just so much honour, when thou yield'st to me,
　　Will waste, as this flea's death took life from thee.

JOHN DONNE

A letter from Wolfgang Amadeus Mozart to his cousin (and probable first love) Marianne

MANNHEIM, 5 NOVEMBER, 1777

Dearest cozz buzz!

I have received reprieved your highly esteemed writing biting, and I have noted doted that my uncle garfuncle, my aunt slant, and you too, are all well mell. We, too, thank god, are in good fettle kettle. Today I got a letter setter from my Papa Haha safely into my paws claws. I hope you too have gotten rotten my note quote that I wrote to you from Mannheim. So much the better, better the much so! But now for some thing more sensuble.

So sorry to hear that Herr Abbate Salate has had another stroke choke. But I hope with the help of God fraud the consequences will not be dire mire. You are writing fighting that you keep your criminal promise which you gave me before my departure from Augspurg, and will do it soon moon. Well, I will most likely find that regretable. You write further, indeed you let it all out, you expose yourself, you indicate to me, you bring me the news, you announce onto me, you state in broad daylight, you demand, you desire, you wish you want, you like, you command that I, too, should send you my Portrait. Eh bien, I shall mail fail it for sure. Oui, by the love of my skin, I shit on your nose, so it runs down your chin.

apropós. do you also have the spuni cuni fait?—what?—whether you still love me?—I believe it! so much the better, better the much so! Yes, that's the way of the world, I'm told, one has the purse, the other has the gold; whom do you side with?—with me, n'est-ce pas?—I believe it! Now things are even worse, apropós.

Wouldn't you like to visit Herr Gold-smith again?—but what for?—what?—nothing!—just to inquire, I guess, about the Spuni Cuni fait, nothing else, nothing else?—well, well, all right. Long live all those who, who—who—who—how does it go on?—I now wish you a good night, shit in your bed with all your might, sleep with peace on your mind, and try to kiss your own behind; I now go off to never-never land and sleep as much as I can stand. Tomorrow we'll speak freak sensubly with each other. Things I must you tell a lot of, believe it you hardly can, but hear tomorrow it already will you, be well in the meantime. Oh my arse burns like fire! what on earth is the meaning of this!—maybe muck wants to come out? yes, yes, muck, I know you, see you, taste you—and—what's this—is it possible? Ye Gods!—Oh ear of mine, are you deceiving me?—No, it's true—what a long and melancholic sound!—today is the write I fifth this letter. Yesterday I talked with the stern Frau Churfustin, and tomorrow, on the 6th, I will give a performance in her chambers, as the Furstin-Chur said to me herself. Now for something real sensuble!

A letter or letters addressed to me will come into your hands, and I must beg of you—where?—well a fox is no hare—yes there!—Now, where was I?—oh yes, now, I remember: letters, letters will come—but what kind of letters?—well now, letters for me, of course, I want to make sure that you send these to me; I will let you know where I'll be going from Mannheim. Now, Numero 2: I'm asking you, why not?—I'm asking you, dearest numbskull, why not?—if you are writing anyway to Madame Tavernier in Munich, please include regards from me to the Mademoiselles Freysinger, why not?—Curious! why not?—and to the Younger, I mean Frauline Josepha, tell her I'll send my sincere apologies, why not?—why should I not apologize?—Curious!—I don't know why not?—I want to apologize that I haven't yet sent her the sonata that I promised, but I will send it as soon as possible, why not?—what—why not?—why shouldn't I send it?—why should I not transmit it?—why not?—Curious! I wouldn't know why not?—well, then you'll do me this favour;—why not?—why shouldn't you do this for me?—why not?, it's so strange! After all, I'll do it to you too, if you want me to, why not?—why shouldn't I do it to you?—curious! why not?—I wouldn't know why not?—and don't forget to send my Regards to the Papa and Mama of the 2 young ladies, for it is terrible to be letting and forgetting one's father and mother. Later, when the sonata is finished,—I will send you the same, and a letter to boot; and you will be so kind as to forward the same to Munich.

And now I must close and that makes me morose. Dear Herr Uncle, shall we go quickly to the Holy Cross Covent and see whether anybody is still up?—we won't stay long, just ring the bell, that's all. Now I must relate to you a sad story that happened just this minute. As I am in the middle of my best writing, I hear a noise in the street. I stop writing—get up, go to the window—and—the noise is gone—I sit down again, start writing once more—I have barely written ten words when I hear the noise again—I rise—but as I rise, I can still hear something but very faint—it smells like something burning—wherever I go it stinks, when I look out the window, the smell goes away, when I turn my head back to the room, the smell comes back—finally My Mama says to me: I bet you let one go?—I don't think so, Mama. yes, yes, I'm quite certain, I put it to the test, stick my finger in my arse, then put it to my nose, and—there is the proof! Mama was right!

Now farwell, I kiss you 10000 times and I remain as always your

Old young Sauschwanz
Wolfgang Amadé Rosenkranz
From us two Travelers a thousand
Regards to my uncle and aunt.
To every good friend I send
My greet feet; addio nitwit.
Love true true true until the grave,
If I live that long and do behave.

Wolfgang Amadeus Mozart

Maria Anna 'Marianne' Thekla Mozart was Mozart's first cousin, the daughter of his father Leopold's younger brother. The two met in 1777 when Marianne was 19 and Wolfgang was 21, and it is thought that their friendship developed into a young love affair. It was all over by the year 1781. Only Mozart's letters remain of their correspondence, striking in their outspoken, surprisingly scatological humour. Indeed, there is speculation as to whether Mozart suffered from Tourette's syndrome. Although Mozart later married Constanze Weber, Marianne was never to marry. It is thought that she continued to carry a torch for her cousin - after her death a portrait that the composer had sent her in 1778 was discovered in her estate.

When a man has married a wife

When a Man has Married a Wife
he finds out whether
Her knees and elbows are only
glued together.

WILLIAM BLAKE

A letter from G.K.Chesterton to his fiancée Frances Blogg

1900?

...I am looking over the sea and endeavouring to reckon up the estate I have to offer you. As far as I can make out my equipment for starting on a journey to fairyland consists of the following items.

1st. A Straw Hat. The oldest part of this admirable relic shows traces of pure Norman work. The vandalism of Cromwell's soldiers has left us little of the original hat-band.

2nd. A Walking Stick, very knobby and heavy: admirably fitted to break the head of any denizen of Suffolk who denies that you are the noblest of ladies, but of no other manifest use.

3rd. A copy of Walt Whitman's poems, once nearly given to Salter, but quite forgotten. It has his name in it still with an affectionate inscription from his sincere friend Gilbert Chesterton. I wonder if he will ever have it.

4th. A number of letters from a young lady, containing everything good and generous and loyal and holy and wise that isn't in Walt Whitman's poems.

5th. An unwieldy sort of a pocket knife, the blades mostly having an edge of a more varied and picturesque outline than is provided by the prosaic cutler. The chief element however is a thing 'to take stones out of a horse's hoof.' What a beautiful sensation of security it gives one to reflect that if one should ever have money enough to buy a horse and should happen to buy one and the horse should happen to have stone in his hoof--that one is ready; one stands prepared, with a defiant smile!

6th. Passing from the last miracle of practical foresight, we come to a box of matches. Every now and then I strike one of these, because fire is beautiful and burns your fingers. Some people think this waste of matches: the same people who object to the building of Cathedrals.

7th. About three pounds in gold and silver, the remains of one of Mr. Unwin's bursts of affection: those explosions of spontaneous love for myself, which, such is the perfect order and harmony of his mind, occur at startingly exact intervals of time.

8th. A book of Children's Rhymes, in manuscript, called the 'Weather Book' about 3/4 finished, and destined for Mr. Nutt. I have been working at it fairly steadily, which I think jolly creditable under the circumstances. One can't put anything interesting in it. They'll understand those things when they grow up.

9th. A tennis racket--nay, start not. It is a part of the new regime, and the only new and neat-looking thing in the Museum. We'll soon mellow it---like the straw hat. My brother and I are teaching each other lawn tennis.

10th. A soul, hitherto idle and omnivorous but now happy enough to be ashamed of itself.

11th. A body, equally idle and quite equally omnivorous, absorbing tea, coffee, claret, sea-water, and swimming. I think, the sea being a convenient size.

12th. A Heart--mislaid somewhere. And that is about all the property of which an inventory can be made at present. After all, my tastes are stoically simple. A straw hat, a stick, a box of matches and some of his own poetry. What more does man require?...

G.K. Chesterton

Wise and witty, G.K. Chesterton was a much celebrated intellectual. He was a prolific writer of poetry, plays, novels, short stories and journalism and is rightly famed as a brilliant wordsmith. On marriage he wrote, 'Marriage is a duel to the death which no man of honour should decline.' He was touchingly romantic on acceptance of his own marriage proposal, writing to his beloved Frances, 'I never knew what being happy meant before tonight.'

To -,

When I loved you, I can't but allow
    I had many an exquisite minute;
But the scorn that I feel for you now
    Hath even more luxury in it!

Thus, whether we're on or we're off,
    Some witchery seems to await you;
To love you was pleasant enough,
    And, oh! 'tis delicious to hate you!

THOMAS MOORE

Recuerdo

We were very tired, we were very merry—
We had gone back and forth all night on the ferry.
It was bare and bright, and smelled like a stable—
But we looked into a fire, we leaned across a table,
We lay on a hill-top underneath the moon;
And the whistles kept blowing, and the dawn came soon.

We were very tired, we were very merry—
We had gone back and forth all night on the ferry;
And you ate an apple, and I ate a pear,
From a dozen of each we had bought somewhere;
And the sky went wan, and the wind came cold,
And the sun rose dripping, a bucketful of gold.

We were very tired, we were very merry,
We had gone back and forth all night on the ferry.
We hailed, 'Good morrow, mother!' to a shawl-covered head,
And bought a morning paper, which neither of us read;
And she wept, 'God bless you!' for the apples and pears,
And we gave her all our money but our subway fares.

EDNA ST VINCENT MILLAY

Symptom Recital

I do not like my state of mind;
I'm bitter, querulous, unkind.
I hate my legs, I hate my hands,
I do not yearn for lovelier lands.
I dread the dawn's recurrent light;
I hate to go to bed at night.
I snoot at simple, earnest folk.
I cannot take the gentlest joke.
I find no peace in paint or type.
My world is but a lot of tripe.
I'm disillusioned, empty-breasted.
For what I think, I'd be arrested.
I am not sick, I am not well.
My quondam dreams are shot to hell.
My soul is crushed, my spirit sore;
I do not like me any more.
I cavil, quarrel, grumble, grouse.
I ponder on the narrow house.
I shudder at the thought of men...
I'm due to fall in love again.

DOROTHY PARKER

One Perfect Rose

A single flow'r he sent me, since we met.
  All tenderly his messenger he chose;
Deep-hearted, pure, with scented dew still wet
  One perfect rose.

I knew the language of the floweret;
  'My fragile leaves,' it said, 'his heart enclose.'
Love long has taken for his amulet
  One perfect rose.

Why is it no one ever sent me yet
  One perfect limousine, do you suppose?
Ah no, it's always just my luck to get
  One perfect rose.

DOROTHY PARKER

may i feel said he

may i feel said he
(i'll squeal said she
just once said he)
it's fun said she

(may i touch said he
how much said she
a lot said he)
why not said she

(let's go said he
not too far said she
what's too far said he
where you are said she)

may i stay said he
(which way said she
like this said he
if you kiss said she

may i move said he
is it love said she)
if you're willing said he
(but you're killing said she

but it's life said he
but your wife said she
now said he)
ow said she

(tiptop said he
don't stop said she
oh no said he)
go slow said she

(cccome? said he
ummm said she)
you're divine! said he
(you are Mine said she)

E. E. CUMMINGS

A Subaltern's Love Song

Miss J. Hunter Dunn, Miss J. Hunter Dunn,
Furnish'd and burnish'd by Aldershot sun,
What strenuous singles we played after tea,
We in the tournament – you against me!

Love-thirty, love-forty, oh! weakness of joy,
The speed of a swallow, the grace of a boy,
With carefullest carelessness, gaily you won,
I am weak from your loveliness, Joan Hunter Dunn.

Miss Joan Hunter Dunn, Miss Joan Hunter Dunn,
How mad I am, sad I am, glad that you won,
The warm-handled racket is back in its press,
But my shock-headed victor, she loves me no less.

Her father's euonymus shines as we walk,
And swing past the summer-house, buried in talk,
And cool the verandah that welcomes us in
To the six-o'clock news and a lime-juice and gin.

The scent of the conifers, sound of the bath,
The view from my bedroom of moss-dappled path,
As I struggle with double-end evening tie,
For we dance at the Golf Club, my victor and I.

On the floor of her bedroom lie blazer and shorts,
And the cream-coloured walls are be-trophied with sports,
And westering, questioning settles the sun,
On your low-leaded window, Miss Joan Hunter Dunn.

The Hillman is waiting, the light's in the hall,
The pictures of Egypt are bright on the wall,
My sweet, I am standing beside the oak stair
And there on the landing's the light on your hair.

By roads 'not adopted', by woodlanded ways,
She drove to the club in the late summer haze,
Into nine-o'clock Camberley, heavy with bells
And mushroomy, pine-woody, evergreen smells.

Miss Joan Hunter Dunn, Miss Joan Hunter Dunn,
I can hear from the car park the dance has begun,
Oh! full Surrey twilight! importunate band!
Oh! strongly adorable tennis-girl's hand!

Around us are Rovers and Austins afar,
Above us, the intimate roof of the car,
And here on my right is the girl of my choice,
With the tilt of her nose and the chime of her voice.

And the scent of her wrap, and the words never said,
And the ominous, ominous dancing ahead.
We sat in the car park till twenty to one
And now I'm engaged to Miss Joan Hunter Dunn.

JOHN BETJEMAN

In the Night

I longed for companionship rather,
But my companions I always wished farther.
And now in the desolate night
I think only of the people I should like to bite.

STEVIE SMITH

⚘ Life Story ⚘

After you've been to bed together for the first time,
without the advantage or disadvantage of any prior acquaintance,
the other party very often says to you,
Tell me about yourself, I want to know all about you,
what's your story? And you think maybe they really and truly do

sincerely want to know your life story, and so you light up
a cigarette and begin to tell it to them, the two of you
lying together in completely relaxed positions
like a pair of rag dolls a bored child dropped on a bed.

You tell them your story, or as much of your story
as time or a fair degree of prudence allows, and they say,
    Oh, oh, oh, oh, oh,
each time a little more faintly, until the oh
is just an audible breath, and then of course

there's some interruption. Slow room service comes up
with a bowl of melting ice cubes, or one of you rises to pee
and gaze at himself with mild astonishment in the bathroom mirror.
And then, the first thing you know, before you've had time
to pick up where you left off with your enthralling life story,
they're telling you *their* life story, exactly as they'd intended to all along,

and you're saying, Oh, oh, oh, oh, oh,
each time a little more faintly, the vowel at last becoming
no more than an audible sigh,
as the elevator, halfway down the corridor and a turn to the left,
draws one last, long, deep breath of exhaustion
and stops breathing forever. Then?

Well, one of you falls asleep
and the other one does likewise with a lighted cigarette in his mouth,
and that's how people burn to death in hotel rooms.

TENNESSEE WILLIAMS

No Loser, No Weeper

'I hate to lose something,'
        then she bent her head
'even a dime, I wish I was dead.
I can't explain it. No more to be said.
Cept I hate to lose something.'

'I lost a doll once and cried for a week.
She could open her eyes, and do all but speak.
I believe she was took, by some doll-snatching-sneak
I tell you, I hate to lose something.'

'A watch of mine once, got up and walked away.
It had twelve numbers on it and for the time of day.
I'll never forget it and all I can say
Is I really hate to lose something.'

'Now if I felt that way bout a watch and a toy,
What you think I feel bout my lover-boy?
I ain't threatening you madam, but he is my evening's joy.
And I mean I really hate to lose something.'

MAYA ANGELOU

Celia, Celia

When I am sad and weary
When I think all hope has gone
When I walk along High Holborn
I think of you with nothing on.

ADRIAN MITCHELL

Valentine

My heart has made its mind up
And I'm afraid it's you.
Whatever you've got lined up,
My heart has made its mind up
And if you can't be signed up
This year, next year, will do.
My heart has made its mind up
And I'm afraid it's you.

WENDY COPE

Mrs Icarus

I'm not the first or the last
to stand on a hillock,
watching the man she married
prove to the world
he's a total, utter, absolute, Grade A pillock.

CAROL ANN DUFFY

Things That Could Happen

1.
She swoons, falls into his arms
and they live together happily ever after.

2.
She kisses him: the restaurant applauds.

3.
There's a pin-drop silence. She turns
the knife in her hand, slowly.

4.
His heart bursts in his mouth before he can say the words.
It splatters the table, ruins her dress, and she never forgives him.

5.
He's interrupted by a handsome man from another table
who asks if he can cut in. She accepts, of course,
and waltzes off to an orchestra of cutlery, side-plates,
strummed napkins and warm bread. He seethes, turns bald
and tells the story to every man he meets.

6.
She falls in love with the waiter.

7.
She falls in love with the waitress.

8.
She starts by saying she's quitting the country,
that there's nothing in London to keep her.

9.
He loses his voice, has to write it all down.
She spills a glass of wine, the ink blurs and swims
across the page. *I'm sorry* she says, and he nods,
his eyes turning to crystal.

10.
They laugh.

11.
They have passionate sex in the single toilet.
Outside, a lengthening queue tuts and frets.
Someone presses their ear to the door.

12.
She doesn't believe him.

13.
They have 3 children. Some nights, she tells them
(again) how their father won her heart
over chicken gyoza and ebi katsu.
Whenever he hears this, something in him rises
like a bull-chested spinnaker.

14.
Her mobile rings. The moment falls, like a crumb,
to the napkin in her lap. She brushes it away.

15.
He learns a new language - says it in French or Swahili.
She's mightily impressed, but doesn't understand.

16.
She chokes on a noodle. The tips of her fingers turn blue
as she fights for breath, and fails. Later, he learns to love
the bite of alcohol and numbs his tongue with ice.

17.
She chokes on a noodle. He Heimlichs her.
She sees him in a different light,
as he dabs the sparkling sputum
from her lips.

18.
He watches the way she eats
and thinks better of saying anything.

19.
Before he can speak, she leans across the table,
fingers barely touching the corners of his mouth,
and says *I know, already. I know.*

JACOB SAM-LA ROSE

.

If Thwarted

'For my part, I prefer my
heart to be broken. It is so lovely,
dawn-kaleidoscopic within the crack.'

D. H. LAWRENCE, FROM 'POMEGRANATE'

Mother, I cannot mind my wheel

Mother, I cannot mind my wheel;
 My fingers ache, my lips are dry;
Oh! if you felt the pain I feel!
 But oh, who ever felt as I!

SAPPHO
(TRANSLATED BY WALTER SAVAGE LANDOR)

Westron wind, when will thou blow

Westron wind, when wilt thou blow,
The small rain down can rain?
Christ if my love were in my arms,
And I in my bed again.

ANONYMOUS

Whoso List To Hunt

Whoso list to hunt, I know where is an hind,
But as for me, alas, I may no more.
The vain travail hath wearied me so sore,
I am of them that furthest come behind.
Yet may I by no means my wearied mind
Draw from the deer; but as she fleeth afore
Fainting I follow. I leave off therefore,
Since in a net I seek to hold the wind.
Who list her hunt, I put him out of doubt,
As well as I may spend his time in vain.
And graven with diamonds in letters plain
There is written, her fair neck round about,
'*Noli me tangere*, for Caesar's I am,
And wild for to hold, though I seem tame.'

SIR THOMAS WYATT

The Nymph's Reply to the Shepherd

If all the world and love were young,
And truth in every shepherd's tongue,
These pretty pleasures might me move
To live with thee and be thy love.

Time drives the flocks from field to fold,
When rivers rage and rocks grow cold,
And Philomel becometh dumb;
The rest complains of cares to come.

The flowers do fade, and wanton fields
To wayward winter reckoning yields;
A honey tongue, a heart of gall,
Is fancy's spring, but sorrow's fall.

Thy gowns, thy shoes, thy beds of roses,
Thy cap, thy kirtle, and thy posies
Soon break, soon wither, soon forgotten,
In folly ripe, in reason rotten.

Thy belt of straw and ivy buds,
Thy coral clasps and amber studs,
All these in me no means can move
To come to thee and be thy love.

But could youth last and love still breed,
Had joys no date nor age no need,
Then these delights my mind might move
To live with thee and be thy love.

SIR WALTER RALEIGH

Sonnet 98

(FROM YOU I HAVE BEEN ABSENT IN THE SPRING)

From you have I been absent in the spring,
When proud pied April, dressed in all his trim,
Hath put a spirit of youth in everything,
That heavy Saturn laughed, and leaped with him.
Yet nor the lays of birds, nor the sweet smell
Of different flowers in odour and in hue,
Could make me any summer's story tell,
Or from their proud lap pluck them where they grew;
Nor did I wonder at the lily's white,
Nor praise the deep vermilion in the rose;
They were but sweet, but figures of delight,
Drawn after you, you pattern of all those.
 Yet seemed it winter still, and, you away,
 As with your shadow I with these did play.

WILLIAM SHAKESPEARE

The Definition of Love

My love is of a birth as rare
As 'tis for object strange and high:
It was begotten by Despair
Upon Impossibility.

Magnanimous Despair alone
Could show me so divine a thing,
Where feeble Hope could ne'er have flown,
But vainly flapped its tinsel wing.

And yet I quickly might arrive
Where my extended soul is fixed,
But Fate does iron wedges drive,
And always crowds itself betwixt.

For Fate with jealous eye does see
Two perfect loves, nor lets them close:
Their union would her ruin be,
And her tyrannic pow'r depose.

And therefore her decrees of steel
Us as the distant poles have placed,
(Though Love's whole world on us doth wheel)
Not by themselves to be embraced,

Unless the giddy heaven fall,
And earth some new convulsion tear;
And, us to join, the world should all
Be cramp'd into a planisphere.

As lines, so loves oblique may well
Themselves in every angle greet;
But ours so truly parallel,
Though infinite, can never meet.

Therefore the love which us doth bind,
But Fate so enviously debars,
Is the conjunction of the mind,
And opposition of the stars.

ANDREW MARVELL

Thrice Toss These Oaken Ashes

Thrice toss these oaken ashes in the air,
Thrice sit thou mute in this enchanted chair;
Then thrice three times tie up this true love's knot.
And murmur soft 'She will, or she will not.'

Go burn these poisonous weeds in yon blue fire,
These screech-owl's feathers and this prickling briar,
This cypress gathered at a dead man's grave,
That all my fears and cares an end may have.

Then come, you fairies, dance with me a round;
Melt her hard heart with your melodious sound.
In vain are all the charms I can devise;
She hath an art to break them with her eyes.

THOMAS CAMPION

The Sick Rose

O Rose thou art sick.
The invisible worm,
That flies in the night
In the howling storm:

Has found out thy bed
Of crimson joy:
And his dark secret love
Does thy life destroy.

WILLIAM BLAKE

She lay all naked

She lay all naked in her bed,
  And I myself lay by;
No veil but curtains about her spread,
  No covering but I:
Her head upon her shoulders seeks
  To hang in careless wise,
And full of blushes was her cheeks,
  And of wishes were her eyes.

Her blood still fresh into her face,
  As on a message came,
To say that in another place
  It meant another game;
Her cherry lip moist, plump, and fair,
  Millions of kisses crown,
Which ripe and uncropped dangle there,
  And weigh the branches down.

Her breasts, that welled so plump and high
  Bred pleasant pain in me,
For all the world I do defy
  The like felicity;
Her thighs and belly, soft and fair,
  To me were only shown:
To have seen such meat, and not to have eat,
  Would have angered any stone.

Her knees lay upward gently bent,
  And all lay hollow under,
As if on easy terms, they meant
  To fall unforced asunder;
Just so the Cyprian Queen did lie,
  Expecting in her bower;
When too long stay had kept the boy
  Beyond his promised hour.

'Dull clown,' quoth she, 'why dost delay
   such proffered bliss to take?
Canst thou find out no other way
   Similitudes to make?'
Mad with delight I thundering
   Throw my arms about her,
But pox upon't 'twas but a dream.
   And so I lay without her.

ANONYMOUS

Never Seek to Tell thy Love

Never seek to tell thy love,
Love that never told can be;
For the gentle wind does move
Silently, invisibly.

I told my love, I told my love.
I told her all my heart;
Trembling, cold, in ghastly fears,
Ah! she doth depart.

Soon as she was gone from me,
A traveller came by,
Silently, invisibly:
He took her with a sigh.

WILLIAM BLAKE

Oh, Dear! What Can The Matter Be?

Oh, dear! What can the matter be? Johnny's so long at the fair!
He promised to buy me a trinket to please me!
And then for a smile, Oh he vowed he would tease me.
He promised to bring me a bunch of blue ribbons to tie up my bonnie brown hair.

He promised to bring me a basket of posies,
A garland of lilies, a gift of red roses,
A little straw hat to set off the blue ribbons that tie up my bonnie brown hair!
Oh dear, what can the matter be? Johnny's so long at the fair!

ANONYMOUS

La Belle Dame sans Merci

O what can ail thee, knight-at-arms,
          Alone and palely loitering?
The sedge has withered from the lake,
          And no birds sing.

O what can ail thee, knight-at-arms,
          So haggard and so woe-begone?
The squirrel's granary is full,
          And the harvest's done.

I see a lily on thy brow,
          With anguish moist and fever-dew,
And on thy cheeks a fading rose
          Fast withereth too.

I met a lady in the meads,
          Full beautiful - a faery's child,
Her hair was long, her foot was light,
          And her eyes were wild.

I made a garland for her head,
          And bracelets too, and fragrant zone;
She looked at me as she did love,
          And made sweet moan.

I set her on my pacing steed,
          And nothing else saw all day long,
For sidelong would she bend, and sing
          A faery's song.

She found me roots of relish sweet,
          And honey wild, and manna-dew,
And sure in language strange she said -
          'I love thee true'.

She took me to her elfin grot,
        And there she wept and sighed full sore,
And there I shut her wild wild eyes
        With kisses four.

And there she lullèd me asleep
        And there I dreamed - Ah! woe betide! -
The latest dream I ever dreamt
        On the cold hill side.

I saw pale kings and princes too,
        Pale warriors, death-pale were they all;
They cried - 'La Belle Dame sans Merci
        Thee hath in thrall!'

I saw their starved lips in the gloam,
        With horrid warning gapèd wide,
And I awoke and found me here,
        On the cold hill's side.

And this is why I sojourn here
        Alone and palely loitering,
Though the sedge is withered from the lake,
        And no birds sing.

JOHN KEATS

To Mary

I sleep with thee, and wake with thee,
And yet thou art not there;
I fill my arms with thoughts of thee,
And press the common air.
Thy eyes are gazing upon mine,
When thou art out of sight;
My lips are always touching thine,
At morning, noon, and night.

I think and speak of other things
To keep my mind at rest:
But still to thee my memory clings
Like love in woman's breast.
I hide it from the world's wide eye,
And think and speak contrary;
But soft the wind comes from the sky,
And whispers tales of Mary.

The night wind whispers in my ear,
The moon shines on my face;
A burden still of chilling fear
I find in every place.
The breeze is whispering in the bush,
And the leaves fall from the tree,
All sighing on, and will not hush,
Some pleasant tales of thee.

JOHN CLARE

❧ Longing ❧

Come to me in my dreams, and then
By day I shall be well again.
For then the night will more than pay
The hopeless longing of the day.

Come, as thou cam'st a thousand times,
A messenger from radiant climes,
And smile on thy new world, and be
As kind to others as to me!

Or, as thou never cam'st in sooth,
Come now, and let me dream it truth,
And part my hair, and kiss my brow,
And say - *My love why sufferest thou?*

Come to me in my dreams, and then
By day I shall be well again.
For then the night will more than pay
The hopeless longing of the day.

MATTHEW ARNOLD

The Shortest and Sweetest of Songs

Come
Home.

GEORGE MACDONALD

If you were coming in the fall

If you were coming in the Fall,
I'd brush the Summer by
With half a smile, and half a spurn,
As Housewives do, a Fly.

If I could see you in a year,
I'd wind the months in balls -
And put them each in separate Drawers,
For fear the numbers fuse -

If only Centuries, delayed,
I'd count them on my Hand,
Subtracting, till my fingers dropped
Into Van Dieman's land.

If certain, when this life was out,
That yours and mine, should be -
I'd toss it yonder, like a Rind,
And take Eternity -

But, now, uncertain of the length
Of this, that is between,
It goads me, like the Goblin Bee,
That will not state - its sting.

EMILY DICKINSON

A letter from David Grier *to* Anna Grier

NOV 10TH 1863
TUESDAY NIGHT

My Darling Wife

My last Letter was written you on Sunday Evening and according to my usual custom I seat myself to write you again. I have now fixed on it to write you a Letter every Sunday, Tuesday + Thursday or Friday, sometimes the former and sometimes the latter day just as circumstances may direct. Do you not think this will be doing very well. I intend to continue doing this as long as I can. We may happen to be sent off somewhere where it will be impossible to get any letters sent away, then of course I shall write whenever I can find an opportunity to send of the Mail. I do not wish you my dear Wife to consider it a task or a duty for me to write you, far from it, it is with a great deal of pleasure that I write you and I must confess that I look forward to the days when I am to write you with a vast amount of pleasure. Yesterday we had quite a change in the Weather. it became suddenly quite cold, and today it is very cold for this country and I had to hunt up a Stove, cut a hole in my Tent for the Pipe, and start a roaring fire. I am in hopes that this will Kill all these Musquitoes which have been troubling us so much of late. Since I last wrote you we have not been favored with a mail, but I am in hopes that the next Boat will bring us one and I shall expect to find for me several Letters from you.

There are a great many rumours afloat as to our future destination We heard a day or two since that one division of our Corps had landed at Point Isabel in Texas. This is situated at the mouth of the Rio Grande and the opposite of the River is held by the French in Mexico. Another Division of our Corps passed through here yesterday on their Road to Brashear City where they are to embark on Steamers for the Rio Grande. Some say that our whole Corps are to go there and that our Division goes next, while others say that only the two divisions go, and the balance of the corps are to stay around here and hold this Country. We as yet have no orders of any Kind and Know nothing as to our future destination. I am strongly in hopes that we are not to be sent to the Rio Grande. I should like very well to see how Mexico looked, and also to take a peep at the French, but it is a long way from home and from you my dear Wife, and I do not care about being so far away from you. I am sure I am far enough now and I feel lonely enough without getting a thousand or so miles farther away from you. I am getting along with the Regiment very well. I drill them about two hours every day and they are improving very fast. I never saw the Men in better health and spirits and they all feel ready to go anywhere or anyplace. We have not a Sick man in the Hospital and our Surgeons are growing fat and lazy for want of something to do. Our Division is rather Small now owing to the other Brigade losing so many men in the fight they had the other day. I feel very lonely and homesick without you and do not Know how I would stand it if it were not for the great Kindness and respect with which the whole Regiment treat me. There is not an officer or man in the Regiment but what would do anything I asked them and that too with the greatest willingness. I do not like myself to say it, but they fairly love me – I am so glad that it is so, for I can manage them as easy as I could a child. What I say to them is law and Gospel, no man every thinks of disputing a word of mine. I of course feel well over all this and it would certainly be hard for me to leave them. I Know that they would dislike very much to have me leave, for now when I talk of doing so, there is quite a breeze generally raised, but still I must leave for although I think a great deal of the 77th but I love my darling wife a great deal more and I would give up any and every thing to be with you. I try by working and studying hard every day to Keep my thoughts away from home, but I find that there is no use trying my mind is constantly on you and I can not live without you. I am continually trying to imagine what you are doing, but of course can not tell anything about it. To morrow is just four weeks since I left you these four weeks have been the longest to me that I ever experienced. on Thursday it will be Eight weeks since we were married. Do you not begin to feel like an old married Woman. How do you get along these cold Nights. I imagine you have a hard time Keeping your Hands and Feet from freezing, don't you remember how I used to try to warm them for you. I do wish I were with you now to render you what assistance I had in my power. I tell you Anna it was always a great pleasure for me to be doing something that would in any way add to your comfort and happiness and I now feel lost, that I can do nothing for you, and I am so afraid that while I am so far away from you, that you will feel the want of my attentions. You Know that I would do any and every thing for you and would consider myself well repaid, by seeing that you were benefited thereby, and that you were happy with me. I Know very well that you love me dearly and would do anything for me, and I am happy in this feeling, but I do feel that all this time that I am seperated from you is just that much time and happiness lost –

I am strong in the hopes that we will get another mail to morrow, and then I shall look for several letters from you. I hope I may not be disappointed.

Good Night my darling Wife. Be sure and write often and rest assured that I will remain always Your Affectionate + Devoted Husband

D.P. Grier

P.S. I have read this Letter over and almost feel ashamed to send it. I see quite a number of mistakes +C. but you must over-look all, for my sake

D.P.G.

General David Grier was forced to spend most of his engagement and the first years of his marriage apart from Anna because of the American Civil War. David survived the war and he and Anna went on to have seven children, and live together until his death.

A Thunderstorm in Town

She wore a new 'terra-cotta' dress,
And we stayed, because of the pelting storm,
Within the hansom's dry recess,
Though the horse had stopped; yea, motionless
    We sat on, snug and warm.

Then the downpour ceased, to my sharp sad pain,
And the glass that had screened our forms before
Flew up, and out she sprang to her door:
I should have kissed her if the rain
    Had lasted a minute more.

THOMAS HARDY

A Broken Appointment

You did not come,
And marching Time drew on, and wore me numb. -
Yet less for loss of your dear presence there
Than that I thus found lacking in your make
That high compassion which can overbear
Reluctance for pure lovingkindness' sake
Grieved I, when, as the hope-hour stroked its sum,
You did not come.

You love not me,
And love alone can lend you loyalty;
- I know and knew it. But, unto the store
Of human deeds divine in all but name,
Was it not worth a little hour or more
To add yet this: Once you, a woman, came
To soothe a time-torn man; even though it be
You love not me.

THOMAS HARDY

from Tess of the D'Urbevilles

Clare came close, and bent over her. 'Dead, dead, dead!' he murmured.

After fixedly regarding her for some moments with the same gaze of unmeasurable woe he bent lower, enclosed her in his arms, and rolled her in the sheet as in a shroud. Then lifting her from the bed with as much respect as one would show to a dead body, he carried her across the room, murmuring -

'My poor, poor Tess - my dearest, darling Tess! So sweet, so good, so true!'

The words of endearment, withheld so severely in his waking hours, were inexpressibly sweet to her forlorn and hungry heart. If it had been to save her weary life she would not, by moving or struggling, have put an end to the position she found herself in. Thus she lay in absolute stillness, scarcely venturing to breathe, and, wondering what he was going to do with her, suffered herself to be borne out upon the landing.

'My wife - dead, dead!' he said.

He paused in his labours for a moment to lean with her against the banister. Was he going to throw her down? Self-solicitude was near extinction in her, and in the knowledge that he had planned to depart on the morrow, possibly for always, she lay in his arms in this precarious position with a sense rather of luxury than terror. If they could only fall together, and both be dashed to pieces, how fit, how desirable.

However, he did not let her fall, but took advantage of the support of the handrail to imprint a kiss upon her lips - lips in the daytime scorned.

THOMAS HARDY

A letter from Oscar Wilde *to* Lord Alfred Douglas

COURTFIELD GARDENS, 20 MAY 1895

My child,

Today it was asked to have the verdicts rendered separately. Taylor is probably being judged at this moment, so that I have been able to come back here. My sweet rose, my delicate flower, my lily of lilies, it is perhaps in prison that I am going to test the power of love. I am going to see if I cannot make the bitter warders sweet by the intensity of the love I bear you. I have had moments when I thought it would be wiser to separate. Ah! Moments of weakness and madness! Now I see that I would have mutilated my life, ruined my art, broken the musical chords which make a perfect soul. Even covered with mud I shall praise you, from the deepest abysses I shall cry to you. In my solitude you will be with me. I am determined not to revolt but to accept every outrage through devotion to love, to let my body be dishonoured so long as my soul may always keep the image of you. From your silken hair to your delicate feet you are perfection to me. Pleasure hides love from us, but pain reveals it in its essence. O dearest of created things, if someone wounded by silence and solitude comes to you, dishonoured, a laughing-stock, Oh! you can close his wounds by touching them and restore his soul which unhappiness had for a moment smothered. Nothing will be difficult for you then, and remember, it is that hope which makes me live, and that hope alone. What wisdom is to the philosopher, what God is to his saint, you are to me. To keep you in my soul, such is the goal of this pain which men call life. O my love, you whom I cherish above all things, white narcissus in an unmown field, think of the burden which falls to you, a burden which love alone can make light. But be not saddened by that, rather be happy to have filled with an immortal love the soul of a man who now weeps in hell, and yet carries heaven in his heart. I love you, I love you, my heart is a rose which your love has brought to bloom, my life is a desert fanned by the delicious breeze of your breath, and whose cool springs are your eyes; the imprint of your little feet makes valleys of shade for me, the odour of your hair is like myrrh, and wherever you go you exhale the perfumes of the cassia tree.

Love me always, love me always. You have been the supreme, the perfect love of my life; there can be no other.

I decided that it was nobler and more beautiful to stay. We could not have been together. I did not want to be called a coward or a deserter. A false name, a disguise, a hunted life, all that is not for me, to whom you have been revealed on that high hill where beautiful things are transfigured.

O sweetest of all boys, most loved of all loves, my soul clings to your soul, my life is your life, and in all the world of pain and pleasure you are my ideal of admiration and joy.

Oscar

Oscar Wilde was married with two sons when he met Lord Alfred Douglas (nicknamed Bosie), but the two soon began an affair. Douglas' vanity and selfishness made the relationship a turbulent one, however. Wilde nursed him back to health when he fell ill from influenza, but when Wilde in turn fell ill, Douglas moved out into the Grand Hotel and charged the bill to Wilde. In 1895, Wilde was arrested on suspicion of homosexual activity.

His relationship with Douglas formed a central part of the trial, and Wilde was convicted and served two years' hard labour. He emerged from prison deeply psychologically changed, and his relationship with Douglas lasted only a few months after his release. After Wilde's death, Douglas turned against him and condemned his homosexuality, although he is said to have relented a little in later years.

The Cap and Bells

The jester walked in the garden:
The garden had fallen still;
He bade his soul rise upward
And stand on her window-sill.

It rose in a straight blue garment,
When owls began to call:
It had grown wise-tongued by thinking
Of a quiet and light footfall;

But the young queen would not listen;
She rose in her pale night-gown;
She drew in the heavy casement
And pushed the latches down.

He bade his heart go to her,
When the owls called out no more;
In a red and quivering garment
It sang to her through the door.

It had grown sweet-tongued by dreaming
Of a flutter of flower-like hair;
But she took up her fan from the table
And waved it off on the air.

'I have cap and bells,' he pondered,
'I will send them to her and die';
And when the morning whitened
He left them where she went by.

She laid them upon her bosom,
Under a cloud of her hair,
And her red lips sang them a love-song
Till stars grew out of the air.

She opened her door and her window,
And the heart and the soul came through,
To her right hand came the red one,
To her left hand came the blue.

They set up a noise like crickets,
A chattering wise and sweet,
And her hair was a folded flower
And the quiet of love in her feet.

W. B. YEATS

The Love Song of St Sebastian

I would come in a shirt of hair
I would come with a lamp in the night
And sit at the foot of your stair;
I would flog myself until I bled,
And after hour on hour of prayer
And torture and delight
Until my blood should ring the lamp
And glisten in the light;
I should arise your neophyte
And then put out the light
To follow where you lead,
To follow where your feet are white
In the darkness toward your bed
And where your gown is white
And against your gown your braided hair.
Then you would take me in
Because I was hideous in your sight
You would take me in without shame
Because I should be dead
And when the morning came
Between your breasts should lie my head.

I would come with a towel in my hand
And bend your head beneath my knees;
Your ears curl back in a certain way
Like no one's else in all the world.
When all the world shall melt in the sun,
Melt or freeze,
I shall remember how your ears were curled.
I should for a moment linger
And follow the curve with my finger
And your head beneath my knees –
I think that at last you would understand.
There would be nothing more to say.
You would love me because I should have strangled you
And because of my infamy;
And I should love you the more because I had mangled you
And because you were no longer beautiful
To anyone but me.

T. S. ELIOT

Call It a Good Marriage

Call it a good marriage -
For no one ever questioned
Her warmth, his masculinity,
Their interlocking views;
Except one stray graphologist
Who frowned in speculation
At her h's and her s's,
His p's and w's.

Though few would still subscribe
To the monogamic axiom
That strife below the hip-bones
Need not estrange the heart,
Call it a good marriage:
More drew those two together,
Despite a lack of children,
Than pulled them apart.

Call it a good marriage:
They never fought in public,
They acted circumspectly
And faced the world with pride;
Thus the hazards of their love-bed
Were none of our damned business -
Till as jurymen we sat on
Two deaths by suicide.

ROBERT GRAVES

Lament over Love

I hope my chile'll
Never love a man.
I say I hope my chile'll
Never love a man.
Cause love can hurt you
Mo'n anything else can.

I'm goin' down to de river
An' I ain't goin' there to swim.
Going down to de river,
Ain't goin' there to swim.
Ma true love's left me, an'
I'm goin' there to think about him.

Love is like whiskey,
Love is like red, red wine.
Love is like whiskey,
O, like sweet red wine.
If you wants to be happy
You got to love all de time.

I'm goin' up in a tower
Tall as a tree is tall.
Say up in a tower
Tall as a tree is tall.
Gonna think about ma man an'
Let ma fool self fall.

LANGSTON HUGHES

Boots of Spanish Leather

Oh, I'm sailin' away my own true love
I'm sailin' away in the morning
Is there something I can send you from across the sea
From the place that I'll be landing?

No, there's nothin' you can send me, my own true love
There's nothin' I wish to be ownin'
Just carry yourself back to me unspoiled
From across that lonesome ocean

Oh, but I just thought you might want something fine
Made of silver or of golden
Either from the mountains of Madrid
Or from the coast of Barcelona

Oh, but if I had the stars from the darkest night
And the diamonds from the deepest ocean
I'd forsake them all for your sweet kiss
For that's all I'm wishin' to be ownin'

That I might be gone a long time
And it's only that I'm askin'
Is there something I can send you to remember me by
To make your time more easy passin'

Oh, how can, how can you ask me again
It only brings me sorrow
The same thing I want from you today
I would want again tomorrow

I got a letter on a lonesome day
It was from her ship a-sailin'
Saying I don't know when I'll be comin' back again
It depends on how I'm a-feelin'

Well, if you, my love, must think that-a-way
I'm sure your mind is roamin'
I'm sure your heart is not with me
But with the country to where you're goin'

So take heed, take heed of the western wind
Take heed of the stormy weather
And yes, there's something you can send back to me
Spanish boots of Spanish leather

BOB DYLAN

❧ Into My Arms ❧

FROM THE ALBUM *THE BOATMAN'S CALL*

I don't believe in an interventionist God
But I know, darling, that you do
But if I did I would kneel down and ask Him
Not to intervene when it came to you
Oh not to touch a hair on your head
Leave you as you are
If He felt He had to direct you
Then direct you into my arms

Into my arms, oh Lord
Into my arms, oh Lord
Into my arms, oh Lord
Into my arms

And I don't believe in the existence of angels
But looking at you I wonder if that's true
And if I did I would summon them together
Ask them to watch over you
To each burn a candle for you
To make bright and clear your path
And to walk, like Christ, in grace and love
And guide you into my arms

Into my arms, oh Lord
Into my arms, oh Lord
Into my arms, oh Lord
Into my arms

But I believe in love
And I know that you do too
And I believe in some kind of path
That we can walk down, me and you
So keep your candles burning
Make a journey bright and pure
That you'll keep returning
Always and evermore

Into my arms, oh Lord
Into my arms, oh Lord
Into my arms, oh Lord
Into my arms

NICK CAVE

Talking in Bed

Talking in bed ought to be easiest,
Lying together there goes back so far,
An emblem of two people being honest.

Yet more and more time passes silently.
Outside, the wind's incomplete unrest
Builds and disperses clouds about the sky,

And dark towns heap up on the horizon.
None of this cares for us. Nothing shows why
At this unique distance from isolation

It becomes still more difficult to find
Words at once true and kind,
Or not untrue and not unkind.

PHILIP LARKIN

'Morning without you
is a dwindled dawn.'

EMILY DICKINSON

So we'll go no more a roving

So, we'll go no more a roving
  So late into the night,
Though the heart be still as loving,
  And the moon be still as bright.

For the sword outwears its sheath,
  And the soul wears out the breast,
And the heart must pause to breathe,
  And love itself have rest.

Though the night was made for loving,
  And the day returns too soon,
Yet we'll go no more a roving
  By the light of the moon.

GEORGE GORDON, LORD BYRON

When We Two Parted

When we two parted
　In silence and tears,
Half broken-hearted
　To sever for years,
Pale grew thy cheek and cold,
　Colder thy kiss;
Truly that hour foretold
　Sorrow to this.

The dew of the morning
　Sunk chill on my brow -
It felt like the warning
　Of what I feel now.
Thy vows are all broken,
　And light is thy fame;
I hear thy name spoken,
　And share in its shame.

They name thee before me,
　A knell to mine ear;
A shudder comes o'er me -
　Why wert thou so dear?
They know not I knew thee,
　Who knew thee too well -
Long, long shall I rue thee,
　Too deeply to tell.

In secret we met -
　In silence I grieve,
That thy heart could forget,
　Thy spirit deceive.
If I should meet thee
　After long years,
How should I greet thee? -
　With silence and tears.

GEORGE GORDON, LORD BYRON

When the lamp is shattered

When the lamp is shattered,
The light in the dust lies dead -
  When the cloud is scattered,
The rainbow's glory is shed.
  When the lute is broken,
Sweet tones are remembered not;
  When the lips have spoken,
Loved accents are soon forgot.

  As music and splendour
Survive not the lamp and the lute,
  The heart's echoes render
No song when the spirit is mute: -
  No song but sad dirges,
Like the wind through a ruined cell,
  Or the mournful surges
That ring the dead seaman's knell.

  When hearts have once mingled,
Love first leaves the well-built nest;
  The weak one is singled
To endure what it once possessed.
  O Love! who bewailest
The frailty of all things here,
  Why choose you the frailest
For your cradle, your home, and your bier?

  Its passions will rock thee
As the storms rock the ravens on high;
  Bright reason will mock thee,
Like the sun from a wintry sky.
  From thy nest every rafter
Will rot, and thine eagle home
  Leave thee naked to laughter,
When leaves fall and cold winds come.

PERCY BYSSHE SHELLEY

❧ Neutral Tones ❧

We stood by a pond that winter day,
And the sun was white, as though chidden of God,
And a few leaves lay on the starving sod;
    – They had fallen from an ash, and were grey.

Your eyes on me were as eyes that rove
Over tedious riddles of years ago;
And some words played between us to and fro
    On which lost the more by our love.

The smile on your mouth was the deadest thing
Alive enough to have strength to die;
And a grin of bitterness swept thereby
    Like an ominous bird a-wing....

Since then, keen lessons that love deceives,
And wrings with wrong, have shaped to me
Your face, and the God-curst sun, and a tree,
    And a pond edged with greyish leaves.

THOMAS HARDY

He would not stay for me; and who can wonder?

He would not stay for me, and who can wonder?
    He would not stay for me to stand and gaze.
I shook his hand, and tore my heart in sunder,
    And went with half my life about my ways.

A.E. HOUSMAN

Down By The Salley Gardens

Down by the salley gardens my love and I did meet;
She passed the salley gardens with little snow-white feet.
She bid me take love easy, as the leaves grow on the tree;
But I, being young and foolish, with her would not agree.

In a field by the river my love and I did stand,
And on my leaning shoulder she laid her snow-white hand.
She bid me take life easy, as the grass grows on the weirs;
But I was young and foolish, and now am full of tears.

W. B. YEATS

O Do Not Love Too Long

Sweetheart, do not love too long:
I loved long and long,
And grew to be out of fashion,
Like an old song.

All through the years of our youth
Neither could have known
Their own thought from the other's,
We were so much at one.

But O, in a minute she changed -
O do not love too long,
Or you will grow out of fashion
Like an old song.

W. B. YEATS

When You Are Old

When you are old and grey and full of sleep,
And nodding by the fire, take down this book,
And slowly read, and dream of the soft look
Your eyes had once, and of their shadows deep;

How many loved your moments of glad grace,
And loved your beauty with love false or true,
But one man loved the pilgrim soul in you,
And loved the sorrows of your changing face;

And bending down beside the glowing bars,
Murmur, a little sadly, how Love fled
And paced upon the mountains overhead
And hid his face amid a crowd of stars.

W.B. YEATS

'Go now'

Like the touch of rain she was
On a man's flesh and hair and eyes
When the joy of walking thus
Has taken him by surprise:

With the love of the storm he burns,
He sings, he laughs, well I know how,
But forgets when he returns
As I shall not forget her 'Go now'.

Those two words shut a door
Between me and the blessed rain
That was never shut before
And will not open again.

EDWARD THOMAS

Will You Come?

Will you come?
Will you come?
Will you ride
So late
At my side?
O, will you come?

Will you come?
Will you come
If the night
Has a moon,
Full and bright?
O, will you come?

Would you come?
Would you come?
If the noon
Gave light,
Not the moon?
Beautiful, would you come?

Would you have come?
Would you have come
Without scorning,
Had it been
Still morning?
Beloved, would you have come?

If you come
Haste and come.
Owls have cried;
It grows dark
To ride.
Beloved, beautiful, come.

EDWARD THOMAS

On Joy and Sorrow

Then a woman said, Speak to us of Joy and Sorrow.

And he answered:

Your joy is your sorrow unmasked.

And the selfsame well from which your laughter rises was oftentimes filled with your tears.

And how else can it be?

The deeper that sorrow carves into your being, the more joy you can contain.

Is not the cup that holds your wine the very cup that was burned in the potter's oven?

And is not the lute that soothes your spirit, the very wood that was hollowed with knives?

When you are joyous, look deep into your heart and you shall find it is only that which has given you sorrow that is giving you joy.

When you are sorrowful, look again in your heart, and you shall see that in truth you are weeping for that which has been your delight.

Some of you say, 'Joy is greater than sorrow,' and others say, 'Nay, sorrow is the greater.'

But I say unto you, they are inseparable.

Together they come, and when one sits alone with you at your board, remember that the other is asleep upon your bed.

Verily you are suspended like scales between your sorrow and your joy.

Only when you are empty are you at standstill and balanced.

When the treasure-keeper lifts you to weigh his gold and his silver, needs must your joy or your sorrow rise or fall.

KAHLIL GIBRAN, FROM *THE PROPHET*

Sonnet II

(TIME DOES NOT BRING RELIEF; YOU ALL HAVE LIED)

Time does not bring relief; you all have lied
Who told me time would ease me of my pain!
I miss him in the weeping of the rain;
I want him at the shrinking of the tide;
The old snows melt from every mountain-side,
And last year's leaves are smoke in every lane;
But last year's bitter loving must remain
Heaped on my heart, and my old thoughts abide!

There are a hundred places where I fear
To go,—so with his memory they brim!
And entering with relief some quiet place
Where never fell his foot or shone his face
I say, 'There is no memory of him here!'
And so stand stricken, so remembering him!

EDNA ST VINCENT MILLAY

⮜ Ebb ⮞

I know what my heart is like
   Since your love died:
It is like a hollow ledge
Holding a little pool
   Left there by the tide,
   A little tepid pool,
Drying inward from the edge.

EDNA ST VINCENT MILLAY

One Cigarette

No smoke without you, my fire.
After you left,
your cigarette glowed on in my ashtray
and sent up a long thread of such quiet grey
I smiled to wonder who would believe its signal
of so much love. One cigarette
in the non-smoker's tray.
As the last spire
trembles up, a sudden draught
blows it winding into my face.
Is it smell, is it taste?
You are here again, and I am drunk on your tobacco lips.
Out with the light.
Let the smoke lie back in the dark.
Till I hear the very ash
sigh down among the flowers of brass
I'll breathe, and long past midnight, your last kiss.

EDWIN MORGAN

Animals

Have you forgotten what we were like then
when we were still first rate
and the day came fat with an apple in its mouth

it's no use worrying about Time
but we did have a few tricks up our sleeves
and turned some sharp corners

the whole pasture looked like our meal
we didn't need speedometers
we could manage cocktails out of ice and water

I wouldn't want to be faster
or greener than now if you were with me O you
were the best of all my days.

FRANK O'HARA

Pain I Did Not

When my husband left, there was pain I did not
feel, which those who lose the one
who loves them feel. I was not driven
against the grate of a mortal life, but
just the slowly shut gate
of preference. At times, I envied them –
what I saw as the honourable suffering
of one who is thrown against that iron
grille. I think he had come, in private, to
feel he was dying, with me, and if
he had what it took to rip his way out, with his
teeth, then he could be born. And so he went
into another world – this
world, where I do not see or hear him –
and my job is to eat the whole car
of my anger, part by part, some parts
ground down to steel-dust. I like best
the cloth seats, blue-grey, first
car we bought together, long since
marked with the scrubbed stains – drool,
tears, ice-cream, no wounds, but only
the month's blood of release, and the letting
go when the water broke.

SHARON OLDS

'O first of friends!/ Still at my heart,
and ever at my side!'

HOMER, *THE ILIAD*

ᕲ Sonnet 104 ᕴ

(TO ME, FAIR FRIEND, YOU NEVER CAN BE OLD)

To me, fair friend, you never can be old,
For as you were when first your eye I eyed,
Such seems your beauty still. Three winters cold
Have from the forests shook three summers' pride,
Three beauteous springs to yellow autumn turned
In process of the seasons have I seen,
Three April perfumes in three hot Junes burned,
Since first I saw you fresh, which yet art green.
Ah, yet doth beauty, like a dial-hand,
Steal from his figure, and no pace perceived;
So your sweet hue, which methinks still doth stand,
Hath motion, and mine eye may be deceived:
　　For fear of which, hear this, thou age unbred,
　　Ere you were born was beauty's summer dead.

WILLIAM SHAKESPEARE

Travelling

This is the spot:—how mildly does the sun
Shine in between the fading leaves! The air
In the habitual silence of this wood
Is more than silent: and this bed of heath,
Where shall we find so sweet a resting place?
Come!—let me see thee sink into a dream
Of quiet thoughts,—protracted till thine eye
Be calm as water when the winds are gone
And no one can tell whither.—my sweet friend!
We two have had such happy hours together
That my heart melts in me to think of it.

WILLIAM WORDSWORTH

To Wordsworth

Poet of Nature, thou hast wept to know
That things depart which never may return:
Childhood and youth, friendship and love's first glow,
Have fled like sweet dreams, leaving thee to mourn.
These common woes I feel. One loss is mine
Which thou too feel'st, yet I alone deplore.
Thou wert as a lone star, whose light did shine
On some frail bark in winter's midnight roar:
Thou hast like to a rock-built refuge stood
Above the blind and battling multitude:
In honoured poverty thy voice did weave
Songs consecrate to truth and liberty,—
Deserting these, thou leavest me to grieve,
Thus having been, that thou shouldst cease to be.

PERCY BYSSHE SHELLEY

To a Friend Who Sent Me Some Roses

As late I rambled in the happy fields,
　What time the sky-lark shakes the tremulous dew
　From his lush clover covert;—when anew
Adventurous knights take up their dinted shields:
I saw the sweetest flower wild nature yields,
　A fresh-blown musk-rose; 'twas the first that threw
　Its sweets upon the summer: graceful it grew
As is the wand that queen Titania wields.
And, as I feasted on its fragrancy,
　I thought the garden-rose it far excell'd:
But when, O Wells! thy roses came to me
　My sense with their deliciousness was spell'd:
Soft voices had they, that with tender plea
　Whisper'd of peace, and truth, and friendliness unquell'd.

JOHN KEATS

The Arrow And The Song

I shot an arrow into the air,
It fell to earth, I knew not where;
For, so swiftly it flew, the sight
Could not follow it in its flight.

I breathed a song into the air,
It fell to earth, I knew not where;
For who has sight so keen and strong,
That it can follow the flight of song?

Long, long afterward, in an oak
I found the arrow, still unbroke;
And the song, from beginning to end,
I found again in the heart of a friend.

HENRY WADSWORTH LONGFELLOW

Love and Friendship

Love is like the wild rose-briar,
Friendship, like the holly tree.
The holly is dark when the rose-briar blooms,
But which will bloom most constantly?

The wild rose-briar is sweet in spring,
Its summer blossoms scent the air;
Yet wait till winter comes again
And who will call the wild-briar fair?

Then, scorn the silly rose-wreath now,
And deck thee with the holly's sheen,
That, when December blights thy brow,
He still may leave thy garland green.

EMILY BRONTË

Sonnet: I Thank You

I thank you, kind and best beloved friend,
With the same thanks one murmurs to a sister,
When, for some gentle favor, he hath kissed her,
Less for the gifts than for the love you send,
Less for the flowers, than what the flowers convey;
If I, indeed, divine their meaning truly,
And not unto myself ascribe, unduly,
Things which you neither meant nor wished to say,
Oh! tell me, is the hope then all misplaced?
And am I flattered by my own affection?
But in your beauteous gift, methought I traced
Something above a short-lived predilection,
And which, for that I know no dearer name,
I designate as love, without love's flame.

HENRY TIMROD

Polonius' Advice To His Son

Beware of the spoken word! Be wise;
Bury thy thoughts in thy breast;
Nor let thoughts that are unnatural
Be ever in acts expressed.

Be thou courteous and kindly toward all —
Be familiar and vulgar with none;
But the friends thou hast proved in thy need
Hold thou fast till life's mission is done!

Shake not thy faith by confiding
In every new-begot friend,
Beware thou of quarrels — but, in them,
Fight them out to the bitter end.

Give thine ear unto all that would seek it,
But to few thy voice impart;
Receive and consider all censure,
But thy judgment seal in thy heart.

Let thy habit be ever as costly
As thy purse is able to span;
Never gaudy, but rich — for the raiment
Full often proclaimeth the man.

Neither borrow nor lend — oft a loan
Both loseth itself and a friend,
And to borrow relaxeth the thrift
Whereby husbandry gaineth its end.

But lo! above all set this law:
UNTO THYSELF BE THOU TRUE!
Then never toward any canst thou
The deed of a false heart do.

MARK TWAIN, PARAPHRASED FROM *HAMLET*

Go to the limits of your longing

God speaks to each of us as he makes us,
then walks with us silently out of the night.

These are the words we dimly hear:

You, sent out beyond your recall,
go to the limits of your longing.
Embody me.

Flare up like a flame
and make big shadows I can move in.

Let everything happen to you: beauty and terror.
Just keep going. No feeling is final.
Don't let yourself lose me.

Nearby is the country they call life.
You will know it by its seriousness.

Give me your hand.

RAINER MARIA RILKE,
(TRANSLATED BY JOANNA MACY AND ANITA BARROW)

And You, Helen

And you, Helen, what should I give you?
So many things I would give you
Had I an infinite great store
Offered me and I stood before
To choose. I would give you youth,
All kinds of loveliness and truth,
A clear eye as good as mine,
Lands, waters, flowers, wine,
As many children as your heart
Might wish for, a far better art
Than mine can be, all you have lost
Upon the travelling waters tossed,
Or given to me. If I could choose
Freely in that great treasure-house
Anything from any shelf,
I would give you back yourself,
And power to discriminate
What you want and want it not too late,
Many fair days free from care
And heart to enjoy both foul and fair,
And myself, too, if I could find
Where it lay hidden and it proved kind.

EDWARD THOMAS

from The Velveteen Rabbit

'What is REAL?' asked the Rabbit one day, when they were lying side by side near the nursery fender, before Nana came to tidy the room. 'Does it mean having things that buzz inside you and a stick-out handle?'

'Real isn't how you are made,' said the Skin Horse. 'It's a thing that happens to you. When someone loves you for a long, long time, not just to play with, but REALLY loves you, then you become Real.'

'Does it hurt?' asked the Rabbit.

'Sometimes,' said the Skin Horse, for he was always truthful. 'When you are Real you don't mind being hurt.'

'Does it happen all at once, like being wound up,' he asked, 'or bit by bit?'

'It doesn't happen all at once,' said the Skin Horse. 'You become. It takes a long time. That's why it doesn't happen often to people who break easily, or have sharp edges, or who have to be carefully kept. Generally, by the time you are Real, most of your hair has been loved off, and your eyes drop out and you get loose in your joints and very shabby. But these things don't matter at all, because once you are Real you can't be ugly, except to people who don't understand.'

MARGERY WILLIAMS

At First Sight

'Love at first sight,' some say, misnaming
Discovery of twinned helplessness
Against the huge tug of procreation.

But friendship at first sight? This also
Catches fiercely at the surprised heart
So that the cheek blanches and then blushes.

ROBERT GRAVES

Friendship

Such love I cannot analyse;
It does not rest in lips or eyes,
Neither in kisses nor caress.
Partly, I know, it's gentleness

And understanding in one word
Or in brief letters. It's preserved
By trust and by respect and awe.
These are the words I'm feeling for.

Two people, yes, two lasting friends.
The giving comes, the taking ends.
There is no measure for such things.
For this all Nature slows and sings.

ELIZABETH JENNINGS

Love after love

The time will come
when, with elation,
you will greet yourself arriving
at your own door, in your own mirror
and each will smile at the other's welcome,

and say, sit here. Eat.
You will love again the stranger who was your self.
Give wine. Give bread. Give back your heart
to itself, to the stranger who has loved you

all your life, whom you ignored
for another, who knows you by heart.
Take down the love letters from the bookshelf,

the photographs, the desperate notes,
peel your own image from the mirror.
Sit. Feast on your life.

DEREK WALCOTT

If Mourning

'Unable are the loved to die.
For love is immortality.'

EMILY DICKINSON

Sonnet 55

(NOT MARBLE, NOR THE GILDED MONUMENTS)

Not marble, nor the gilded monuments
Of princes, shall outlive this powerful rhyme;
But you shall shine more bright in these contents
Than unswept stone, besmeared with sluttish time.
When wasteful war shall statues overturn,
And broils root out the work of masonry,
Nor Mars his sword, nor war's quick fire, shall burn
The living record of your memory:
'Gainst death and all-oblivious enmity
Shall you pace forth; your praise shall still find room
Even in the eyes of all posterity
That wear this world out to the ending doom.
    So, till the judgement that yourself arise,
      You live in this, and dwell in lovers' eyes.

WILLIAM SHAKESPEARE

❧ Sonnet 71 ☙

(NO LONGER MOURN FOR ME WHEN I AM DEAD)

No longer mourn for me when I am dead
Than you shall hear the surly sullen bell
Give warning to the world that I am fled
From this vile world, with vilest worms to dwell:
Nay, if you read this line, remember not
The hand that writ it, for I love you so,
That I in your sweet thoughts would be forgot,
If thinking on me then should make you woe.
O if (I say), you look upon this verse
When I, perhaps, compounded am with clay,
Do not so much as my poor name rehearse,
But let your love even with my life decay;
  Lest the wise world should look into your moan,
  And mock you with me after I am gone.

WILLIAM SHAKESPEARE

Upon the death of Sir Albert Morton's Wife

He first deceased; she for a little tried
To live without him, liked it not, and died.

SIR HENRY WOTTON

Holy Sonnet 17

(SINCE SHE WHOM I LOV'D HATH PAID HER LAST DEBT)

Since she whom I lov'd hath paid her last debt
To nature, and to hers, and my good is dead,
And her soul early into heaven ravished,
Wholly in heavenly things my mind is set.
Here the admiring her my mind did whet
To seek thee, God; so streams do show the head;
But though I have found thee, and thou my thirst hast fed,
A holy thirsty dropsy melts me yet.
But why should I beg more love, whenas thou
Dost woo my soul, for hers off'ring all thine,
And dost not only fear lest I allow
My love to saints and angels, things divine,
But in thy tender jealousy dost doubt
Lest the world, flesh, yea devil put thee out.

JOHN DONNE

On My First Son

Farewell, thou child of my right hand, and joy;
My sin was too much hope of thee, lov'd boy.
Seven years tho' wert lent to me, and I thee pay,
Exacted by thy fate, on the just day.
O, could I lose all father now! For why
Will man lament the state he should envy?
To have so soon 'scap'd world's and flesh's rage,
And if no other misery, yet age?
Rest in soft peace, and, ask'd, say, 'Here doth lie
Ben Jonson his best piece of poetry.'
For whose sake henceforth all his vows be such,
As what he loves may never like too much.

BEN JONSON

The last letter from from Lord Nelson to Lady Hamilton

(THIS LETTER WAS DISCOVERED ON NELSON'S DESK AFTER HE WAS KILLED AT THE BATTLE OF TRAFALGAR)

VICTORY, 19 OCTOBER 1805, NOON; CADIZ, ESE 16 LEAGUES

My dearest beloved Emma, the dear friend of my bosom - The signal has been made that the Enemy's Combined Fleet is coming out of port. We have very little wind, so that I have no hopes of seeing them before to-morrow. May the God of Battles crown my endeavours with success! At all events I shall take care that my name shall ever be most dear to you and Horatia, both of whom I love as much as my own life; and as my last writing before the battle will be to you, so I hope in God that I shall live to finish my letter after the Battle. May Heaven keep you, prays your Nelson & Bronte.

October 20th. In the morning we were close to the Mouth of the Straights, but the wind had not come far enough to the Westward to allow the Combined Fleets to weather the Shoals off Trafalgar, but they were counted as far as forty Sail of Ships of War which I suppose to be thirty-four of the Line and six Frigates. A group of them was seen off the Lighthouse of Cadiz this morning, but it blows so very fresh, I think... that I rather believe they will go into the Harbour before night.

May God Almighty give us success over these fellows and enable us to get a Peace.

Lady Emma Hamilton had no formal education and spent her early years working as a maid, model and actress. Through a string of controversial affairs she met and married Sir William Hamilton, who was 44 years her senior, and was still married to him when she met the (also married) military·commander Horatio Nelson. The two fell in love and struck up an affair under the gaze of the elderly, and surprisingly accommodating, Sir William, which lasted to Nelson's death. The three even lived together, and Emma bore Nelson two children, one of whom died in infancy. After Nelson's death, the provisions which he had attempted to make for Emma were ignored by the government, and she was taken into debtor's prison, eventually dying in poverty in Calais in 1815. On the last of Nelson's letters to her, Emma has scrawled 'Oh, miserable, wretched Emma. Oh glorious and happy Nelson.'

Music when Soft Voices Die (To —)

Music, when soft voices die,
Vibrates in the memory—
Odours, when sweet violets sicken,
Live within the sense they quicken.

Rose leaves, when the rose is dead,
Are heaped for the belovèd's bed;
And so thy thoughts, when thou art gone,
Love itself shall slumber on.

PERCY BYSSHE SHELLEY

A slumber did my spirit seal

A slumber did my spirit seal;
   I had no human fears:
She seemed a thing that could not feel
   The touch of earthly years.

No motion has she now, no force;
   She neither hears nor sees;
Rolled round in earth's diurnal course,
   With rocks, and stones, and trees.

WILLIAM WORDSWORTH

Song: I had a dove

I had a dove and the sweet dove died;
And I have thought it died of grieving:
O, what could it grieve for? Its feet were tied,
With a silken thread of my own hand's weaving:
Sweet little red feet! Why should you die?
Why should you leave me, sweet bird! why?
You liv'd alone in the forest tree,
Why, pretty thing, would you not live with me?
I kiss'd you oft, and gave you white peas;
Why not live sweetly, as in the green trees?

JOHN KEATS

❧ Sonnet 20 ❧

(BELOVED, MY BELOVED)

Belovèd, my Belovèd, when I think
That thou wast in the world a year ago,
What time I sate alone here in the snow
And saw no footprint, heard the silence sink
No moment at thy voice, but, link by link,
Went counting all my chains as if that so
They never could fall off at any blow
Struck by thy possible hand – why, thus I drink
Of life's great cup of wonder! Wonderful,
Never to feel thee thrill the day or night
With personal act or speech, - nor ever cull
Some prescience of thee with the blossoms white
Thou sawest growing! Atheists are as dull,
Who cannot guess God's presence out of sight.

ELIZABETH BARRETT BROWNING

From In Memoriam A.H.H.

Dark house, by which once more I stand
   Here in the long unlovely street,
   Doors, where my heart was used to beat
So quickly, waiting for a hand,

A hand that can be clasp'd no more -
   Behold me, for I cannot sleep,
   And like a guilty thing I creep
At earliest morning to the door.

He is not here; but far away
   The noise of life begins again,
   And ghastly thro' the drizzling rain
On the bald street breaks the blank day.

ALFRED, LORD TENNYSON

On the Death of Anne Brontë

There's little joy in life for me,
    And little terror in the grave;
I've lived the parting hour to see
    Of one I would have died to save.

Calmly to watch the failing breath,
    Wishing each sigh might be the last;
Longing to see the shade of death
    O'er those belovèd features cast.

The cloud, the stillness that must part
    The darling of my life from me;
And then to thank God from my heart,
    To thank Him well and fervently;

Although I knew that we had lost
    The hope and glory of our life;
And now, benighted, tempest-tossed,
    Must bear alone the weary strife.

CHARLOTTE BRONTË

To One Shortly To Die

From all the rest I single out you, having a message for you,
You are to die—Let others tell you what they please, I cannot prevaricate,
I am exact and merciless, but I love you—there is no escape for you.

Softly I lay my right hand upon you, you just feel it,
I do not argue. I bend my head close and half envelop it,
I sit quietly by, I remain faithful,
I am more than nurse, more than parent or neighbor,
I absolve you from all except yourself spiritual bodily, that is eternal,
    you yourself will surely escape,
The corpse you will leave will be but excrementitious.

The sun bursts through in unlooked-for directions.
Strong thoughts fill you and confidence, you smile!
You forget you are sick, as I forget you are sick,
You do not see the medicines, you do not mind the weeping friends, I am
    with you,
I exclude others from you, there is nothing to be commiserated,
I do not commiserate, I congratulate you.

WALT WHITMAN

Remember

Remember me when I am gone away,
    Gone far away into the silent land;
    When you can no more hold me by the hand,
Nor I half turn to go, yet turning stay.
Remember me when no more day by day
    You tell me of our future that you planned:
    Only remember me; you understand
It will be late to counsel then or pray.
Yet if you should forget me for a while
    And afterwards remember, do not grieve:
    For if the darkness and corruption leave
    A vestige of the thoughts that once I had,
Better by far you should forget and smile
    Than that you should remember and be sad.

CHRISTINA ROSSETTI

ᘉ Song ᘒ

When I am dead, my dearest,
Sing no sad songs for me;
Plant thou no roses at my head,
Nor shady cypress tree:
Be the green grass above me
With showers and dewdrops wet;
And if thou wilt, remember,
And if thou wilt, forget.

I shall not see the shadows,
I shall not feel the rain;
I shall not hear the nightingale
Sing on, as if in pain;
And dreaming through the twilight
That doth not rise nor set,
Haply I may remember,
And haply may forget.

CHRISTINA ROSSETTI

Rain on a Grave

Clouds spout upon her
      Their waters amain
      In ruthless disdain, –
Her who but lately
      Had shivered with pain
As at touch of dishonour
If there had lit on her
So coldly, so straightly
      Such arrows of rain:

One who to shelter
      Her delicate head
Would quicken and quicken
      Each tentative tread
If drops chanced to pelt her
      That summertime spills
      In dust-paven rills
When thunder-clouds thicken
      And birds close their bills.

Would that I lay there
      And she were housed here!
Or better, together
Were folded away there
Exposed to one weather
We both, – who would stray there
When sunny the day there,
      Or evening was clear
      At the prime of the year.

Soon will be growing
      Green blades from her mound,
And daisies be showing
      Like stars on the ground,
Till she form part of them –
Ay – the sweet heart of them,
Loved beyond measure
With a child's pleasure
      All her life's round.

THOMAS HARDY

⤳ The Voice ⤲

Woman much missed, how you call to me, call to me,
Saying that now you are not as you were
When you had changed from the one who was all to me,
But as at first, when our day was fair.

Can it be you that I hear? Let me view you, then,
Standing as when I drew near to the town
Where you would wait for me: yes, as I knew you then,
Even to the original air-blue gown!

Or is it only the breeze, in its listlessness
Travelling across the wet mead to me here,
You being ever dissolved to wan wistlessness,
Heard no more again far or near?

Thus I; faltering forward,
Leaves around me falling,
Wind oozing thin through the thorn from norward,
And the woman calling.

THOMAS HARDY

Along the fields as we came by

Along the field as we came by
A year ago, my love and I,
The aspen over stile and stone
Was talking to itself alone.
'Oh who are these that kiss and pass?
A country lover and his lass;
Two lovers looking to be wed;
And time shall put them both to bed,
But she shall lie with earth above,
And he beside another love.'

And sure enough beneath the tree
There walks another love with me,
And overhead the aspen heaves
Its rainy-sounding silver leaves;
And I spell nothing in their stir,
But now perhaps they speak to her,
And plain for her to understand
They talk about a time at hand
When I shall sleep with clover clad,
And she beside another lad.

A. E. HOUSMAN

From a sermon in May 1910 following the death of King Edward VII titled 'Death the King of Terrors'

Death is nothing at all. I have only slipped away to the next room. I am I and you are you.

Whatever we were to each other, that we are still. Call me by my old familiar name. Speak to me in the easy way which you always used. Put no difference into your tone. Wear no forced air of solemnity or sorrow. Laugh as we always laughed at the little jokes we enjoyed together. Play, smile, think of me. Pray for me. Let my name be ever the household word that it always was. Let it be spoken without effect. Without the trace of a shadow on it. Life means all that it ever meant. It is the same that it ever was. There is absolute unbroken continuity. Why should I be out of mind because I am out of sight? I am but waiting for you. For an interval. Somewhere. Very near. Just around the corner. All is well.

HENRY SCOTT HOLLAND

The suicide note from Virginia Woolf to Leonard Woolf

TUESDAY.

Dearest,

I feel certain that I am going mad again. I feel we can't go through another of those terrible times. And I shan't recover this time. I begin to hear voices, and I can't concentrate. So I am doing what seems the best thing to do. You have given me the greatest possible happiness. You have been in every way all that anyone could be. I don't think two people could have been happier till this terrible disease came. I can't fight any longer. I know that I am spoiling your life, that without me you could work. And you will I know. You see I can't even write this properly. I can't read. What I want to say is I owe all the happiness of my life to you. You have been entirely patient with me and incredibly good. I want to say that — everybody knows it. If anybody could have saved me it would have been you. Everything has gone from me but the certainty of your goodness. I can't go on spoiling your life any longer.

I don't think two people could have been happier than we have been.

V.

An Arundel Tomb

Side by side, their faces blurred,
The earl and countess lie in stone,
Their proper habits vaguely shown
As jointed armour, stiffened pleat,
And that faint hint of the absurd—
The little dogs under their feet.

Such plainness of the pre-baroque
Hardly involves the eye, until
It meets his left-hand gauntlet, still
Clasped empty in the other; and
One sees, with a sharp tender shock,
His hand withdrawn, holding her hand.

They would not think to lie so long.
Such faithfulness in effigy
Was just a detail friends would see:
A sculptor's sweet commissioned grace
Thrown off in helping to prolong
The Latin names around the base.

They would not guess how early in
Their supine stationary voyage
The air would change to soundless damage,
Turn the old tenantry away;
How soon succeeding eyes begin
To look, not read. Rigidly they

Persisted, linked, through lengths and breadths
Of time. Snow fell, undated. Light
Each summer thronged the glass. A bright
Litter of birdcalls strewed the same
Bone-riddled ground. And up the paths
The endless altered people came,

Washing at their identity.
Now, helpless in the hollow of
An unarmorial age, a trough
Of smoke in slow suspended skeins
Above their scrap of history,
Only an attitude remains:

Time has transfigured them into
Untruth. The stone fidelity
They hardly meant has come to be
Their final blazon, and to prove
Our almost-instinct almost true:
What will survive of us is love.

PHILIP LARKIN

◦⟁ Red ⟁◦

Red was your colour.
If not red, then white. But red
Was what you wrapped around you.
Blood-red. Was it blood?
Was it red-ochre, for warming the dead?
Haematite to make immortal
The precious heirloom bones, the family bones.

When you had your way finally
Our room was red. A judgement chamber.
Shut casket for gems. The carpet of blood
Patterned with darkenings, congealments.
The curtains - ruby corduroy blood,
Sheer blood-falls from ceiling to floor.
The cushions the same. The same
Raw carmine along the window-seat.
A throbbing cell. Aztec altar - temple.

Only the bookshelves escaped into whiteness.

And outside the window
Poppies thin and wrinkle-frail
As the skin on blood,
Salvias, that your father named you after,
Like blood lobbing from a gash,
And roses, the heart's last gouts,
Catastrophic, arterial, doomed.

Your velvet long full skirt, a swathe of blood,
A lavish burgundy.
Your lips a dipped, deep crimson.

You revelled in red.
I felt it raw - like crisp gauze edges
Of a stiffening wound. I could touch
The open vein in it, the crusted gleam.

Everything you painted you painted white
Then splashed it with roses, defeated it,
Leaned over it, dripping roses,
Weeping roses, and more roses,
Then sometimes, among them, a little bluebird.

Blue was better for you. Blue was wings.
Kingfisher blue silks from San Francisco
Folded your pregnancy
In crucible caresses.
Blue was your kindly spirit - not a ghoul
But electrified, a guardian, thoughtful.

In the pit of red
You hid from the bone-clinic whiteness.

But the jewel you lost was blue.

TED HUGHES

Acknowledgements

'I would maintain that thanks are
the highest form of thought, and that
gratitude is happiness doubled by wonder'

G.K. CHESTERTON

I would like to thank my editor Rosemary Davidson; Ruth Warburton, Kate Bland, Rose McClaren, Rowena Skelton-Wallace and Simon Rhodes at Square Peg, Random House UK; John Garrett, my proofreader; the design team: Emma King, Kristen Harrison and Ramon Dodd at The Curved House and Jonathan Baker at Seagull Design; Eugenie Furniss and Liane-Louise Smith at the literary agency Furniss Lawton; the permissions departments at nearly every publisher of poetry in the English-speaking world; the multiple award winning actors Gina Bellman, Helena Bonham Carter, Tom Hiddleston, Damian Lewis, Helen McCrory and Emma Watson who not only came in to read on *The Love Book* app but also suggested some of the poems here; others who have researched, written and given me a thousand ideas: John Ash, Farah Ghouri, Eleanor Hardy, Maisie Lawrence, Cecily Long, Hannah Phillips, Amy Waite, Becky Watson and James Whittle; Rachel Kelly, my co-editor for the *iF Poems* app and book; Tim Burton and Derek Frey for setting me up with the wonder that is Air Studios; Carol Ann Duffy, Susannah Herbert and William Sieghart for their wit and wisdom about poetry and the poetry world; Richard Curtis for suggesting songs; Sarah Vine for her friendship and writing prowess; Maiken, Jane B, Beatie, Lucy, Henrietta, Anna, Natasha, Jane P, James, Mel, Pidge, Michael, Samantha, Mary and Sam for an awful lot of listening; Venetia Butterfield, Harry Enfield, Emma Freud, Mariella Frostrup, Sian Griffiths, David James, Tom Konig, Alan Parker, Sue Peart and *You* magazine, Kate Reardon, Chrissie Rucker, Samantha Sheffield, Save the Children, Alexandra Shulman, *The Times*, Nick Wheeler, Luke Windsor and David Yelland for advice, support, press and much help pushing poetry; and my husband Mark and our children, Eliza, Rosie and Jack, whom *i carry in my heart*.

The author and publisher gratefully acknowledge permission to reprint copyright material in this book as follows:

MAYA ANGELOU
'Come. And be my baby' from *Oh Pray My Wings Are Going To Fit Me Well* by Maya Angelou (Random House, Inc., 1975), Copyright © 1975 Maya Angelou. 'No Loser, No Weeper' by Maya Angelou from *Just Give Me A Cool Drink Of Water 'Fore I Diiie* © 1971 Maya Angelou. Reprinted by permission of The Helen Brann Agency.

SIMON ARMITAGE
'Let me put it this way' from *Book of Matches* (Faber and Faber, 2001). Reprinted by permission of the publisher.

W.H AUDEN
'Lullaby' and 'Funeral Blues' by W. H. Auden. Copyright © 1940 by W. H. Auden, renewed. Reprinted by permission of Curtis Brown, Ltd.

JOHN BETJEMAN
'A Subaltern's Love Song' by John Betjeman. Copyright ©John Betjeman by permission of the estate of John Betjeman.

ELIZABETH BISHOP
'Close close all night...' by Elizabeth Bishop from *Edgar Allan Poe and the Juke Box* by Elizabeth Bishop, edited and annotated by Alice Quinn. Copyright © 2006 by Alice Helen Methfessel. Reprinted by permission of Farrar, Straus and Giroux, LLC.

NICK CAVE
The lyrics to 'Into My Arms' by Nick Cave from 1997's album *The Boatman's Call* by Nick Cave and The Bad Seeds.

WENDY COPE
'Valentine' and 'The Orange' from *Serious Concerns* (Faber and Faber, 1992) and *Two Cures for Love: Selected Poems, 1979-2006* (Faber and Faber, 2008) respectively. Reprinted by permission of the publisher.

E. E. CUMMINGS
'i carry your heart with me(i carry it in, Copyright 1952, © 1980, 1991 by the trustees of the E.E. Cummings Trust, and 'may i feel said he, Copyright 1935, © 1963, 1991 by the Trustees of the E.E. Cummings Trust. Copyright ©1978 by George J. Firmage, from *Collected Poems: 1904-1962* by E.E. Cummings, edited by George J. Firmage. Used by permission of the Liveright Publishing Corporation.

CAROL ANN DUFFY
'Mrs Icarus' from *The World's Wife* by Carol Ann Duffy. © Carol Ann Duffy 1999. Reproduced with permission from the author care of Picador, London.

'Valentine' from *Mean Time* by Carol Ann Duffy. Copyright © Carol Ann Duffy 1993. Reproduced by permission of the author care of Rogers, Coleridge & White Ltd., 20 Powis Mews, London W11 1JN

'Words, Wide Night' from *The Other Country* by Carol Ann Duffy. © Carol Ann Duffy 2010. Reproduced by permission of the author care of Rogers, Coleridge & White Ltd., 20 Powis Mews, London W11 1JN

BOB DYLAN
Boots of Spanish Leather. Written by

SHARON OLDS
'Pain I Did Not' taken from *Stag's Leap* by Sharon Olds. Published by Jonathan Cape, 2012. Reprinted by permission of The Random House Group Limited.

ALICE OSWALD
'Wedding' from *The Thing in the Gap-Stone Stile* (Faber and Faber, 2007). Reprinted by permission of the publisher.

DOROTHY PARKER
Dorothy Parker 'Symptom Recital' and 'One Perfect Rose' by Dorothy Parker from *The Best of Dorothy Parker* (Gerald Duckworth & Co. Ltd) reprinted by permission of Gerald Duckworth & Co.Ltd.

RAINER MARIA RILKE
'Go to the limits of your longing' by Rainer Maria Rilke, as translated by Anita Barrows and Joanna Macy, reprinted from *The Book of Hours* (Riverhead Books, 2005) with permission from Janklow and Nesbit.

MICHAEL SYMMONS ROBERTS
'The Vows' from *Drysalter* by Michael Symmons Roberts (Jonathan Cape, a division of The Random House Group Ltd). Copyright © Michael Symmons Roberts 2013. Reprinted by permission of the publisher.

ROBIN ROBERTSON
'Tryst's' from *Swithering* by Robin Robertson (Picador, 2006). Copyright © Robin Robertson, 2006. Reprinted by permission of the publisher.

JACOB SAM-LA ROSE
'Things That Could Happen' by Jacob Sam-La Rose from *A Storm Between Fingers* published by Malika's Kitchen (Flipped Eye Publishing Ltd, 2007) and *Penguin's Poems for Love* (Penguin, 2009). Copyright © Jacob Sam-La Rose, 2007, reprinted by permission of the author.

STEVIE SMITH
'Conviction (iv)' and 'Into The Night' from *Collected Poems and Drawings* (Faber and Faber). Reprinted by permission of the publisher.

DYLAN THOMAS
'On the Marriage of a Virgin' by Dylan Thomas, from *The Poems* (Orion). Reprinted by permission of David Higham Associates on behalf of Dylan Thomas.

DEREK WALCOTT
'Love after Love' by Derek Walcott, from *Collected Poems 1948-1984*. Copyright ©1986 by Derek Walcott. Reprinted by permission of Farrar, Straus and Giroux.

TENNESSEE WILLIAMS
'Life Story' from *The Collected Poems of Tennessee Williams* © 1937 by the University of The South. Reprinted by permission of George Borchardt, Inc. for the estate of Tennessee Williams. All rights reserved.

Author Index

Adcock, Fleur (1934 –) 71

Angelou, Maya (1928 –) 33

Anonymous 134, 142, 145

Armitage, Simon (1963 –) 100

Arnold, Matthew (1822 – 1888) 86, 149

Auden, W.H. (1907 – 1973) 26

Barrett Browning, Elizabeth (1806 – 1861) 15, 83, 84, 216

Betjeman, John (1906 – 1984) 120

Bishop, Elizabeth (1911 – 1979) 29

Blake, William (1757 – 1827) 111, 141, 144

Bonaparte, Napoleon (1769 – 1821) 45

Bradstreet, Anne (1612 – 1672) 80

Brontë, Charlotte (1816 – 1855) 218

Brontë, Emily (1818 – 1848) 54, 196

Browning, Robert (1812 – 1889) 52, 53

Burns, Robert (1759 – 1796) 82

Byron, George Gordon (1788 – 1824) 11, 12, 173, 174

Campion, Thomas (1567 – 1620) 140

Catullus (c.84 – c.54 BC) 3

Cave, Nick (1957 –) 168

Chesterton, G.K. (1874 – 1936) 112

Clare, John (1793 – 1864) 13, 148

Coleridge, S.T. (1772 – 1834) 37, 48

Cope, Wendy (1945 –) 34, 126

Cummings, E.E. (1894 – 1962) 95, 118

Curtis, Richard (1956 –) 103

Davies, John (1565 – 1618) 106

Dickens, Charles (1812 – 1870) 1

Dickinson, Emily (1830 – 1886) 23, 57, 58, 151, 171, 205

Donne, John (1572 – 1631) 41, 77, 107, 210

Duffy, Carol Ann (1955 –) 35, 36, 127

Dylan, Bob (1941 –) 166

Eliot, T.S. (1888 – 1965) 93, 162

Elton, Ben (1959 –) 103

Fenton, James (1949 –) 99

Fuller, John (1937 –) 30

Gibran, Kahlil (1883 – 1931) 92, 183

Graves, Robert (1895 – 1985) 164, 202

Grier, David, General (1836 – 1891) 152

Gunn, Thom (1929 – 2004) 70

Hardy, Thomas (1840 – 1928) 73, 155, 156, 157, 176, 222, 224

Heaney, Seamus (1939 – 2013) 98

Henry VIII (1491 – 1547) 4

Herrick, Robert (1591 – 1674) 44

Holland, Henry Scott (1847 – 1918) 226

Housman, A.E. (1859 – 1936) 177, 225

Hughes, Langston (1902 – 1967) 165

Hughes, Ted (1930 – 1998) 68, 230

Jennings, Elizabeth (1926 – 2001) 203

Jonson, Ben (c. 1572 – 1637) 9, 211

Keats, John (1795 – 1821) 14, 16, 50, 146, 194, 215

King James Bible (1611) 10, 78, 79

Larkin, Philip (1922 – 1985) 170, 228

Lawrence, D.H. (1885 – 1930) 64, 90, 131

Lear, Edward (1812 – 1888) 85

Longfellow, Henry Wadsworth (1807 – 1882) 195

Lowell, Amy (1874 – 1925) 61

Macdonald, George (1824 – 1905) 150

Mansfield, Katherine (1888 – 1923) 65, 94

Marlowe, Christopher (1564 – 1593) 5, 40

Marvell, Andrew (1621 – 1678) 42, 138

Mitchell, Adrian (1932 – 2008) 125

Moore, Thomas (1779 – 1852) 114

Morgan, Edwin (1920 –) 186

Mozart, Wolfgang Amadeus (1756 – 1791) 81, 108

Nelson, Lord (1758 – 1805) 212

O'Hara, Frank (1926 – 1966) 187

Olds, Sharon (1942 –) 188

Oswald, Alice (1966 –) 102

Owen, Wilfred (1893 – 1918) 66

Parker, Dorothy (1893 – 1967) 116, 117

Petronius (c. 27 – c. 66 AD) 39

Poe, Edgar Allan (1809 – 1849) 18

Raleigh, Sir Walter (c. 1552 – 1618) 136

Rilke, Rainer Maria (1875 – 1926) 199

Roberts, Michael Symmons (1963 –) 101

Robertson, Robin (1955 –) 72

Roethke, Theodore (1908 – 1963) 28

Rossetti, Christina (1830 – 1894) 22, 220, 221

Rossetti, Dante Gabriel (1828 – 1882) 21

Sam-La Rose, Jacob (1976 –) 128

Sappho (c. 630 – 570 BC) 133

Sayre, Zelda (1900 – 1948) 96

Scott, Sir Walter (1771 – 1832) 46

Shakespeare, William (1564 – 1616) 6, 7, 8, 76, 105, 137, 191, 207, 208

Shelley, Percy Bysshe (1792 – 1822) 49, 175, 193, 213

Sidney, Sir Philip (1554 – 1586) 75

Smith, Stevie (1902 – 1971) 25, 122

St. Vincent Millay, Edna (1892 – 1950) 115, 184, 185

Swinburne, Algernon Charles (1837 – 1909) 59

Tennyson, Alfred, Lord (1809 – 1892) 51, 217

Thomas, Dylan (1914 – 1953) 67

Thomas, Edward (1878 – 1917) 181, 182, 200

Timrod, Henry (1828 – 1867) 197

Twain, Mark (1835 – 1910) 88, 198

Walcott, Derek (1930 –) 204

Whitman, Walt (1819 – 1892) 19, 20, 55, 56, 219

Wilde, Oscar (1854 – 1900) 158

Williams, Margery (1881 – 1944) 201

Williams, Tennessee (1911 – 1983) 123

Wotton, Sir Henry (1568 – 1639) 209

Woolf, Virginia (1882 – 1941) 62, 63, 227

Wordsworth, William (1770 – 1850) 192, 214

Wyatt, Sir Thomas (1503 – 1542) 135

Yeats, W.B. (1865 – 1939) 24, 60, 89, 160, 178, 179, 180

Index of Titles and First Lines of Poems

A Birthday 22

A Broken Appointment 156

A Decade 61

A Dedication To My Wife 93

A Drinking Song 24

A Glimpse 56

A glimpse through an interstice caught 56

A Red, Red Rose 82

A single flow'r he sent me, since we met 117

A slumber did my spirit seal 214

A slumber did my spirit seal 214

A Subaltern's Love Song 120-1

A sudden blow: the great wings beating still 60

A Thunderstorm in Town 155

After you've been to bed together for the first time 123

Along the field as we came by 225

Along the field as we came by 225

An Arundel Tomb 228-9

And You, Helen 200

And you, Helen, what should I give you? 200

Animals 187

As late I rambled in the happy fields 194

At First Sight 202

At lunchtime I bought a huge orange - 34

Bargain, The 75

Bed, The 70

Belovèd, my Belovèd, when I think 216

Beware of the Spoken word! Be Wise 198

Boots of Spanish Leather 166-7

Bride and Groom Lie Hidden for Three Days 68-9

Bright Star 14

Bright Star! would I were steadfast as thou art - 14

Call It a Good Marriage 164

Call it a good marriage - 164

Camomile Tea 94

Cap and Bells, The 160-1

Celia, Celia 125

Close close all night 29

close close all night 29

Clouds spout upon her 222-3

Come Home 150

Come live with me and be my love 40

Come to me in my dreams, and then 149

Come. And Be My Baby 33

Comparison, The 3

Conviction (iv) 25

Coupling 71

Dark house, by which once more I stand 217

Definition of Love, The 138-9

Desire 37, 48

Doing, a filthy pleasure is, and short 39

Doing, a filthy pleasure is, and short 39

Dover Beach 86-7

Down By The Salley Gardens 178
*Down by the salley gardens my love
and I did meet* 178
Drink to me only with thine eyes
9

Ebb 185

Face That Launched A Thousand
Ships, The 5
*Farewell, thou child of my right
hand, and joy* 211
Fidelity 90–1
*Fidelity and love are two different
things, like a flower and a gem*
90–1
*First time he kissed me, he but only
kissed* 15
Flea, The 107
*For my part, I prefer my heart to be
broken* 131
Friendship 203
*From all the rest I single out you,
having a message for you*
219
*From time to time our love is like a
sail* 102
*From you have I been absent in the
spring* 137

*Give me my Romeo; and when I
shall die* 8
'Go now' 181
Go to the limits of your longing
199
*God speaks to each of us as he
makes us* 199
Good Morrow, The 41

*Had I the heavens' embroidered
cloths* 89

Had we but world enough, and time
42–3
*Have you forgotten what we were
like then* 187
*He first deceased; she for a little
tried* 209
He Wishes for the Cloths of Heaven
89
*He would not stay for me, and who
can wonder?* 177
He would not stay for me; and who
can wonder? 177
Helen, thy beauty is to me 18
Her breast is fit for pearls 57
Her breast is fit for pearls 57
Hinterhof 99
Holy Sonnet 17 (Since She Whom I
Lov'd Hath Paid Her Last Debt)
210
*How do I love thee? Let me count
the ways* 84

i carry your heart with me(i carry it
in 95
*i carry your heart with me(i carry it
in* 95
*I cry your mercy, pity, love – ay,
love!* 50
I do not like my state of mind 116
*I don't believe in an interventionist
God* 168–9
*I had a dove and the sweet dove
died* 215
'I hate to lose something,' 124
I hid my love when young till I 13
I hid my love when young till I 13
I hope my chile'll 165
I Knew a Woman 28
I knew a woman, lovely in her bones
28
I know what my heart is like 185

I like to get off with people 25
I longed for companionship rather 122
I shot an arrow into the air 195
I sleep with thee, and wake with thee 148
I thank you, kind and best beloved friend 197
I wonder, by my troth, what thou and I 41
I would come in a shirt of hair 162–3
I'm not the first or the last 127
If all the world and love were young 136
If ever two were one, then surely we 80
If there were, oh! an Hellespont of cream 106
If thou must love me, let it be for nought 83
If yet I have not all thy love 77
If you were coming in the fall 151
If you were coming in the Fall 151
Iliad, The 189
In Memoriam A.H.H. 217
In the Night 122
Into My Arms 168–9
It was a quiet way 23
It was a quiet way – 23

La Belle Dame sans Merci 146–7
Lament over Love 165
Lay your sleeping head, my love 26–7
Leaves Murmuring by myriads in the shimmering trees 66
Leda and the Swan 60
Let me not to the marriage of true minds 76
Let me put it this way 100
Let me put it this way 100

Life Story 123
Like the touch of rain she was 181
Lochinvar 46–7
Longing 149
Love after love 204
Love and Friendship 196
Love and Sleep 59
'Love at first sight,' some say, misnaming 202
Love is like the wild rose-briar 196
Love Song of St Sebastian, The 162–3
Love's Philosophy 49
Lovers' Infiniteness 77
Lullaby 26–7
Lying asleep between the strokes of night 59

Mark but this flea, and mark in this 107
Masons, when they start upon a building 98
may I feel said he 118–19
may I feel said he 118–19
meet me where the sun goes down 72
Meeting at Night 53
Miss J. Hunter Dunn, Miss J. Hunter Dunn 120–1
'Morning without you is a dwindled dawn' 171
Mother, I cannot mind my wheel 133
Mother, I cannot mind my wheel 133
Mrs Icarus 127
Music when Soft Voices Die (To -) 213
Music, when soft voices die 213
My beloved is white and ruddy 10
My Diary 66

My heart has made its mind up 126

My heart is like a singing bird 22

My love is of a birth as rare 138-9

My luve is like a red, red rose 82

My mistress' eyes are nothing like the sun 6

My true love hath my heart, and I have his 75

Neutral Tones 176

Never Seek to Tell thy Love 144

Never seek to tell thy love 144

New Year's Eve 64

No longer mourn for me when I am dead 208

No Loser, No Weeper 124

No smoke without you, my fire 186

Not a red rose or a satin heart 35

Not marble, nor the gilded monuments 207

Now 52

Now sleeps the crimson petal 51

Now sleeps the crimson petal, now the white 51

Nymph's Reply to the Shepherd, The 136

O Do Not Love Too Long 179

O first of friends!/Still at my heart 189

O Rose thou art sick 141

O tan-faced prairie-boy 19

O tan-faced prairie-boy 19

O what can ail thee, knight-at-arms 146-7

O young Lochinvar is come out of the west 46-7

Oh, Dear! What Can The Matter Be? 145

Oh, Dear! What Can The Matter Be? Johnny's so long at the fair! 145

Oh, I'm sailin' away my own true love 166-7

On Joy and Sorrow 183

On Marriage 92

On My First Son 211

On the Death of Anne Brontë 218

On the Marriage of a Virgin 67

On the wall above the bedside lamp 71

One Cigarette 186

One Perfect Rose 117

Orange, The 34

Out of your whole life give but a moment! 52

Outside the sky is light with stars 94

Owl and the Pussy-cat, The 85

Pain I Did Not 188

Passing stranger! you do not know how longingly I look upon you 55

Passionate Shepherd to His Love, The 40

Poet of Nature, thou hast wept to know 193

Polonius' Advice To His Son 198

Pomegranate 131

Rain on a grave 222-3

Recuerdo 115

Red 230-1

Red was your colour 230-1

Remember 220

Remember me when I am gone away 220

Romeo and Juliet 8

Scaffolding 98

Shall I compare thee to a summer's day? 7

She gives him his eyes, she found them 68-9

She lay all naked 142-3

She lay all naked in her bed 142-3

She swoons, falls into his arms 128-30

She Walks in Beauty 11

She walks in beauty, like the night 11

She wore a new 'terra-cotta' dress 155

Shortest and Sweetest of Songs, The 150

Sick Rose, The 141

Side by side, their faces blurred 228-9

Silent Noon 21

Since she whom I lov'd hath paid her last debt 210

So we'll go no more a roving 173

So, we'll go no more a roving 173

Somewhere, on the other side of this wide night 36

Song 221

Song of Solomon 10

Song: I had a dove 215

Sonnet: I Thank You 197

Sonnet 11 (Time Does Not Bring Relief; You All Have Lied) 184

Sonnet 14 (If Thou Must Love Me) 83

Sonnet 18 (Shall I Compare Thee To A Summer's Day?) 7

Sonnet 20 (Belovèd, My Belovèd) 216

Sonnet 38 (First Time He Kissed Me) 15

Sonnet 43 (How Do I Love Thee?) 84

Sonnet 55 (Not Marble, Nor the Gilded Monuments) 207

Sonnet 71 (No Longer Mourn For Me When I Am Dead) 208

Sonnet 98 (From You I Have Been Absent In The Spring) 137

Sonnet 104 (To Me, Fair Friend, You Never Can Be Old) 191

Sonnet 116 (Let Me Not To The Marriage of True Minds) 76

Sonnet 130 (My mistress' eyes are nothing like the sun) 6

Stay near to me and I'll stay near to you – 99

Such love I cannot analyse 203

Sweetheart, do not love too long 179

Symptom Recital 116

Talking in Bed 170

Talking in bed ought to be easiest 170

The Arrow And The Song 195

The Author loving these homely meats specially, viz.: Cream, Pancakes, Buttered Pippin-pies (laugh, good people) and Tobacco: writ to that worthy and virtuous gentlewoman, whom he calleth Mistress, as followeth 106

The crowd of beauteous Quintia prate 3

The fountains mingle with the river 49

The grey sea and the long black land 53

The highway is full of big cars going nowhere fast 33

The jester walked in the garden 160-1

The Owl and the Pussy-cat went to sea 85

The pulsing stops where time has been 70

The sea is calm to-night 86–7

The things about you I appreciate 30–2

The time will come 204

Then a woman said, Speak to us of Joy and Sorrow 183

Then Almitra spoke again and said, 'And what of Marriage, master?' 92

There are only two things now 64

There's little joy in life for me 218

Things That Could Happen 128–30

This is the spot:-how mildly does the sun 192

Thrice Toss These Oaken Ashes 140

Thrice toss these oaken ashes in the air 140

Time does not bring relief; you all have lied 184

To -, 114

To a Friend Who Sent Me Some Roses 194

To a Stranger 55

To Celia 9

To Fanny 50

To Helen 18

To His Coy Mistress 42–3

To Mary 148

To me, dear friend, you can never be old 191

To My Dear and Loving Husband 80

To One Shortly To Die 220

To whom I owe the leaping delight 93

To Wordsworth 193

Travelling 192

Trysts 72

Unable are the loved to die 205

Upon Julia's Clothes 44

Upon the death of Sir Albert Morton's Wife 209

Valentine (Cope) 126

Valentine (Duffy) 35

Valentine (Fuller) 30–2

Voice, The 224

Vows, The 101

Waking alone in a multitude of loves when morning's light 67

Was this the face that launched a thousand ships 5

We pledge to wake each morning face-to-face 101

We stood by a pond that winter day 176

We were very tired, we were very merry 115

Wedding 102

Westron wind, when wilt thou blow 134

Westron wind, when wilt thou blow 134

When a man has married a wife 111

When a Man has Married a Wife 111

When as in silks my Julia goes 44

When I am dead, my dearest 221

When I am sad and weary 125

When I heard at the close of the day 20

When I heard at the close of the day how my name had been receiv'd with 20

When I loved you, I can't but allow 114

When my husband left, there was pain I did not 188
When the lamp is shattered 175
When the lamp is shattered 175
When We Two Parted 174
When we two parted 174
When You Are Old 180
When you are old and grey and full of sleep 180
When you came, you were like red wine and honey 61
Where true Love burns, Desire is Love's pure flame 37, 48
Whoso List To Hunt 135

Whoso list to hunt, I know where is an hind 135
Wild nights – Wild nights! 58
Wild nights – Wild nights! 58
Will You Come? 182
Will you come? 182
Wine comes in at the mouth 24
Woman much missed, how you call to me, call to me, 224
Words. Wide Night 36

You did not come 156
Your hands lie open in the long fresh grass, - 21